MISSIONARY
ONBOARD!

FAITH & WORKS

Yes to Obey, Yes to His Will, Yes to His Way, Yes to Lead, Yes to Follow

NOT MAN BUT GOD!

Sharon Forde-Atikossie

ISBN 978-1-0980-2703-2 (paperback)
ISBN 978-1-0980-7205-6 (hardcover)
ISBN 978-1-0980-2704-9 (digital)

Copyright © 2020 by Sharon Forde-Atikossie

All rights reserved. No part of this publication may be reproduced, distributed, or transmitted in any form or by any means, including photocopying, recording, or other electronic or mechanical methods without the prior written permission of the publisher. For permission requests, solicit the publisher via the address below.

Christian Faith Publishing, Inc.
832 Park Avenue
Meadville, PA 16335
www.christianfaithpublishing.com

Printed in the United States of America

I would like to dedicate this book to my grandmother who was known as Baby Arthur, Martha Arthur, Martha May Ugel, Moda Arthur, or the lady with the donkey cart.

She paved the way for me to be accepted by some of the people during my mission journeys in Guyana, South America, where I grew up.

To my husband, for his prayers, love, and support and for being a true prayer warrior.

CONTENTS

Foreword 7
Acknowledgments 9
Introduction 11
Christian Versus Christianity 13
    Who is a Christian? 13
    What is Christianity? 14
A Mission 16
Christian Mission 17
    Types of Christian missions 19
    The Benefits of Christian Missions 20
Who is a Missionary? 22
    Types of missionaries 23
        Homeland missionaries 23
        Overseas missionaries 23
        Evangelistic missionaries 24
        Need-based missionaries 24
    Roles and duties of a missionary 25
Handbook Instruction for Christian Missionaries 26
    Expectations of a Missionary 27
    Physical and temporal well-being 42
        Transportation 42
        Health 42
    Security 42

Missionary Assignment 44
    Ministering.. 44
    Responsibility while on a mission trip....................... 45
    Meetings.. 45
    Selling of goods 46
    Making promises 46
Information Card 48
Host Country Perception 49
Establishing a Mission Ministry 52
    Mission purpose 52
    Reason for the outreach mission 53
    Decrease in church attendance..................................... 54
Preparation for Mission 57
Researching Information 69
Establishing a Business Checklist... 81
My Grandparents 87
Becoming a Missionary 93
My So-called Break from God 98
Spiritual Biography, Sharon Forde-Atikossie, DMin 101
My Journey 104
My Mission Trip Experiences 106
    Returning to Guyana.. 108
Doing Too Much.. 110
Am I Reaching Lost Souls 112
My Experience Returning Home as a Missionary 115
The Word Faith... 117
    Fully Aligning In True Holiness 117
Missionary Walk with God... 119
The Devil Made Me Do It! 121
Difference in Culture 123
Inequality Treatment of the Missionary 125
Preparing for My Mission Trip 128

Conclusion.. 131
References 133

FOREWORD

It is essential to read this book. The subject matter speaks for itself, for there is a soundness, clarity, power of authority, and the remarkable qualities of the author.

The book shows that the author has enduring qualities and a firm foundation as a missionary.

Her writing shows the extraordinary quality, unique value, dedication, and confidence of a missionary.

The author has a unique value of combining her military experiences and her missionary work, which shows her greatest determination to effectively accomplish her mission work, and that is to draw souls to Christ.

The author shows an inspirational resourcefulness for establishing a mission ministry and going beyond the four walls of the church.

I have the greatest respect and is highly honored to know this woman of God who exhibits her true calling as a missionary.

Her love and faith for God shows constantly, not only in her writing but also in her daily lifestyle.

Rev. Robert Atikossie

ACKNOWLEDGMENTS

To Jesus Christ who is my Savior, my Counselor, and my Redeemer who lives and is the God who is in the driving seat of my life, who shows me daily how to have faith and trust in Him.

To my husband, Robert, for his love and support; to my father, Sydney Forde, who always had a warm smile for me; to my mother, Olive Arthur, for her daily encouraging word and love.

To my brother, Alston, who calls to make sure I am well; to my sister Pamela, who keeps me in her prayer; to my sister June, who always share a burst of laughter; and to my sister Patricia, who is my daily prayer partner.

My son, Fabrice, through his daily dedication and dutifulness to his responsibilities, in reference to his daughter London's welfare, my Tele Fabriena, reminded me of how I should be with my God daily. And not forgetting my younger son Ako Paolo, whom I cannot help but smile and shake my head whenever I look at him, and also the entire Atikossie family who embraced me with their love and who calls me their Queen.

To my Faith and Love Pentecostal Church family, who embraced my family and me and who has the vision to go beyond the four walls of the church.

To Chosen300 Ministry, who gives me the opportunity to continuously work for the Lord.

To my grandmother, Martha Arthur, who has paved the way for me to be accepted during my mission journey in Guyana, South America.

INTRODUCTION

It is evident that there is a lot more work to be done when it comes to acknowledging and knowing who God is.

We find ourselves in an environment where there are too many individuals who do not know Jesus Christ and who have no understanding of the Holy Bible or what it means to live for Jesus Christ.

According to research, over 7,111 documented languages are written and spoken in todays' society, and double of that amount are spoken languages only, and when we look at the Holy Bible, we will find that the Word of God is spoken in over 21,333 languages, yet there are so many unbelievers around us, both domestically and internationally.

Due to this observation, I realized that there is a need to reach out all over the world to draw awareness to the Son of God, and one of the ministries who can join forces with the evangelism and outreach ministry is the mission ministry.

These ministries consist of devoted Christians who are known to be missionaries that have the thirst for going beyond the four walls of the church to not only spread the Gospel but to convert souls to Jesus Christ

CHRISTIAN VERSUS CHRISTIANITY

Please understand that there are differences between a Christian and Christianity. In today's society, both words are used to imply that an individual who is just simply attending a Christian Church is a Christian. For example, one may ask an individual what is their religion, and in most cases, the reply would be, "I am a Christian."

Who is a Christian?

An individual is not a Christian just because they are attending church. They should be someone who believe by faith that the Holy Bible is true, one who surrendered their life to Christ, born of the Holy Spirit, and having that willingness to be obedient to the Word of God, which is the Holy Bible.

They are those who continuously live their life in a Christlike manner, and that they must have faith and believe that there is one true God, where Jesus, the son of God, was sent to earth by his Father where He was crucified and died on the cross for the sins of the world, buried, rose to the heavens, and will come to earth again.

That individual must have faith and believe that God is three in one, who are distinctive and yet equal.

What is Christianity?

We learn that Christianity is a religion. It is based on the teaching of Jesus, the Son of God, who is known as "the anointed one" and that He is divine in nature as well as human, and also based on the miracles that Jesus Christ performed.

Jesus is the anointed one from God the Father who came to this world, fulfilled the Old Testament laws and prophecies, died on the cross, and rose from the dead physically, and also, it relates to the Old Testament and the New Testament.

Some fundamental doctrines of Christianity include:

- *Trinity*. One God in three persons.
- *The Person of Jesus Christ*. Jesus in the form of flesh, fully man and fully God for all eternity.
- *Salvation*. By grace alone, through faith alone in Jesus Christ alone.
- *The Scripture*.

The dictionary describes Christianity as "a monotheistic system of beliefs and practices based on the Old Testament and the teachings of Jesus as embodied in the New Testament, and emphasizing the role of Jesus as savior."

There are many Christianity religions which have similarities in their teaching about Jesus, yet different in many ways. Here are some of them: Catholic, Orthodox, Protestant, Anglicans, the Assyrian Church of the East, the Ancient Church of the East, Evangelical, Anabaptist, Reformist, Lutheran, Great Schism, Eastern Catholic, Eastern Orthodox, Oriental Orthodox, Communion, Restoration, Nontrinitarian, and many others

The main teaching is that God is the Trinity, and that they are three in One that are distinctive and yet equal—"The Father; the Word, the Holy Spirit."

When reading the below books in the Bible, we will see that this is true:

- Romans 8:3
- Isaiah 53:6, 64:6
- Romans 3:32, 6:28
- Colossian 2:13
- 2 Corinthians 5:21
- Romans 6:23
- Matthew 10:28, 23:33
- Ephesians 2:8–9
- 2 Corinthians 5:21

To sum it up, Christianity is a religion which tells us that Jesus Christ will be born of a virgin and will be sacrificed for mankind's sins, and these information are referenced in the Holy Bible over forty-four times.

QUESTION: How would you describe Christianity?
DISCUSSION:_____
_____
_____
_____

A MISSION

A mission is described as an assignment that has to be carried out to accomplish a task. For example, during my tenure in the United States Armed Forces, I was involved with two types of missions.

These missions are known as operational and institutional. Both consisted of specific tasks, and I was expected to accomplish them using the rules and regulations. These were missions that were instructed, and these missions were given because they were vitally important and there is the expectation of some form of results.

QUESTION: Have you ever been on a mission?
DISCUSSION:_____
_____
_____
_____

CHRISTIAN MISSION

When looking at Christian missions, they are not as straightforward as one would believe, and yet they are vitally important.

A Christian mission is a Christian ministry (a body of believers) who is obedient to Jesus Christ, who accepts their primary responsibility to go beyond the four walls of the church to spread the gospel, thereby, drawing souls to Christ through spreading the gospel and solely relying on His Word.

To sum it up, Christian mission is sharing the Word of God with as many people as possible,

These ministry members meet the people where they are with the intent to share the Word of God, with the hope that they will convert them to the true faith which is believing that Jesus Christ died on the cross to save mankind

Christian mission is not a one-man show; it not advisable for only one person to go in the field to do any form of mission. Safety should be their concern. It should be a group of Christians with the sole agenda and responsibility to convert and to draw souls to Jesus Christ.

It is evident in the Holy Bible, especially when looking at Paul the Apostle and his missionary journeys that are seen in the book of Romans, 1 and 2 Corinthians, Galatians, Philippians, 1 and 2 Thessalonians, Philemon, Ephesians, Colossians, 1 and 2 Timothy and Titus and also the other letters Paul has written.

The Holy Bible expressed the true meaning of what a mission is, and that is to go beyond the four walls of the church and give, release, and show mercy to those who are brokenhearted, downtrodden, and in need of mercy and also to spiritually feed the "hungry and give drink to the thirsty."

> Declare his glory among the heathen, his wonders among all people. (Ps. 96:3, KJV)

> For whosoever shall call upon the name of the LORD shall be saved. How then shall they call on him in whom they have not believed? and how shall they believe in him of whom they have not heard? and how shall they hear without a preacher? And how shall they preach, except they be sent? as it is written, How beautiful are the feet of them that preach the gospel of peace, and bring glad tidings of good things! (Rom. 10:13–15, KJV)

When we look at Jesus Christ, His true purpose and mission was to come to earth to die for our sins, to save sinners, to save that which is lost, and for the resurrection after His death.

After His resurrection and return to His Father, His disciples continued to do His work, which is to draw souls through spreading the gospel upon His command.

> After this the LORD appointed seventy-two others and sent them two by two ahead of him to every town and place where he was about to go. (Luke 10:1)

QUESTION: Would you like to experience a Christian Mission?
DISCUSSION:_____

> I learn that mission is the intentional crossing of barriers from Church to non-church in word and deed for the sake of the proclamation of the Gospel. (Stephen Neill)

Types of Christian missions

Christian missions are divided into three categories, and these are:

- Long-term mission (LTM), from three years to the extended time;
- Mid-term missions (MTM), from nine months to two years, and
- Short-term (STM), the time frame ranges from a few days to eight months, and they are also called Mission Trips.

(Note that these time frames vary depending on the church or ministry).

In the case of long-term mission (LTM), this is known to be the backbone of the ministry. The members of this mission are those who delegate their time to set the groundwork of the mission and to keep the mission operational.

They are mostly seasoned Christians who have the experience of a teacher, culturally adaptable, wise in their well-doing, have a positive attitude toward the leaders and the people around them, having the willingness to work under the culture vision, must be accountable, able to receive direction, be a true servant at heart, walk with God's love and share God's love at all times, and be Christlike at all times.

In the case of mid-term mission (MTM), this is the beginning of a preparation period, and some go with a specific task in mind. This is where they have overcome the initial shock of their first visit, and the decision has been made that mission work is for them. Even though evangelism is the primary role, they go with the intent to begin the groundwork and to invest not only in themselves but to engage effectively with the culture and gain knowledge.

When looking at short-term missions (STM), the time frame ranges from a few days to eight months, and they are also called mission trips. These are trips where professionals, students, and other individuals would like to have the experience of going beyond the four walls of the church to spread the gospel. It is also a period where new missionaries get the opportunity to learn about mission work and begin to put into practice what they were trained on and to decide what type of missionary work they would like to choose to work in. Most importantly, those who go on these trips regularly evangelize and get the opportunity to see firsthand of the cultures, languages, and the peoples' ways of life.

QUESTION: What are your suggestions on the various types of missions?
DISCUSSION:_____
_____
_____
_____

The Benefits of Christian Missions

As one knows, the reason for missions is to reach those who do not know who Jesus Christ is, not only to tell them but to teach them about Him. It is an environment that gives the opportunity for children of God to learn hands on and gain various important skills that are required to build a great foundation for the mission.

I learned that missionary trips are becoming a venue for students to gain opportunity for internship, thereby gaining college credit, and missions have become a career field in the secular world.

Missions are known to be team builders, a place to learn new culture, foster the development of leadership skills. Missions provide opportunities for learning new things daily, exploring different types of possibilities, learning from others, one-on-one coaching, and building deep relationships.

QUESTION: Have you been a missionary? List other benefits you would like to see.

DISCUSSION:_____
_____
_____
_____

WHO IS A MISSIONARY?

A missionary is someone within the body of Christ who works in spreading the gospel of Jesus Christ beyond the four walls of the church.

> Missionaries are Christian workers who engage in cross-cultural ministries with evangelistic goals. (C. Peter Wagner)
>
> A missionary is a prepared disciple whom God sends into the world with his resources to make disciples for his Kingdom. (Ada Lum, *A Hitchhiker's Guide to Missions*)
>
> A Christian missionary is a person whose passion is to make the Lord Jesus known to the whole world. I believe that "being a missionary" in the truest sense of the word is taking the Gospel where it has never been before, or at least to a different culture or a different language group.
> A true missionary is someone who will risk everything for the sake of the loss of the world. (Keith Green)

They can be leaders and laypersons in the church, and depending on the church's policy, missionaries can be anointed positions.

Note! Jesus was a missionary at heart, and He is a true missionary.

However it is a calling on one's life, it is something that God does, calling the individual to Him.

Types of missionaries

Types of missionaries can be broken down into categories such as homeland missionaries, overseas missionaries, evangelistic missionaries, and need-based missionaries.

Homeland missionaries

Homeland missionaries are children of God who work solely at home, from within the church, and they work within the neighborhood, devoting themselves to a specific mission purpose. They would also send items to various places. For example, someone who is a member of a church, who has never traveled overseas, can collect items and ship them to various places to support the need of others. They are considered missionaries, and it does not matter their position in the church.

Overseas missionaries

Overseas missionaries are those who travel abroad or live in foreign countries. They often go to evangelize and help people in need. In most cases, they are a part of a nonprofit group or religious organization. They help to raise support and prayer for the missionaries' efforts.

Evangelistic missionaries

Evangelistic missionaries are those whose main objective is to convert the individual to their religion. The focus of their work is to preach and teach in areas where the people may have never heard before who Jesus Christ is. These are people who try to reach out to as many as possible individuals through door-to-door activities, holding crusades, holding meetings to talk about Jesus, and organizing various committee socials.

Note that while many evangelistic missionaries are involved in some aspect of helping people in need, their main objective is to spread the gospel of Jesus Christ with the intent to draw them to Him.

Need-based missionaries

Need-based missionaries are those who focus mainly on helping people in different areas. Evangelism is a part of their service, but meeting the needs of the people become their primary objective. This type of missionaries plant churches, build churches, establish orphanages, establish schools, provide logistics, distribute medical supplies, and provide food and water and clothing for the need of the people.

Some of the missionaries, especially short-term missionaries, fall into this category because they use their professional skills to assist, such as doctors, builders, dentist, and professions that suit the needs of the people.

QUESTION: Which one of the above duties would you like to experience?

DISCUSSION: _____

_____

_____

Roles and duties of a missionary

Sharing the Gospel. The primary role of missionaries is to use every moment and opportunity available to them to serve as witnesses for Christ. This is done through teaching others about Jesus Christ, and this may be done formally, through sermons and lectures, or informally, by talking one-on-one with others.

Training groups. This is having the responsibility in providing training to other Christians in various areas visited to share their common beliefs with others so that that the missionary work becomes continuous.

Community building: These are the need-based missionaries, who utilize their education and skill sets in varying ways during a mission.

Report back. Missionaries are responsible for reporting back to their ministry, sometimes, in the form of report or discussion to their church or ministry.

QUESTION: Please add other roles and duties a missionary should have.
DISCUSSION: _____
_____
_____
_____

HANDBOOK INSTRUCTION FOR CHRISTIAN MISSIONARIES

Below are some of the things that a missionary needs to know prior to traveling, during mission trips and preparations prior to returning from the mission trip and upon returning from the mission trip

Depending on the type of trip, a missionary may or may not get a thorough briefing, however, they should use common sense. If they do not know something or think they do not know, it is better to be safe than sorry and ask the missionary leader, for being obedient is the key. The Bible tell us in Proverbs, "Keep your heart with all vigilance, for from it flow the springs of life" (Proverbs 4:23, ESV).

Always remember the Ten Commandments, for a missionary must always strive to embrace the companionship of the Holy Spirit and follow God's direction in living these principles and standards.

A missionary must always remember that they are, officially, representatives of God, the mission ministry, their church, and themselves. Being so, they are expected to maintain the highest standards of conduct and appearance by keeping the commandments.

Expectations of a Missionary

Missionaries are expected to follow the rules, regulations, and procedures of the mission leader. While on the mission trip, they are also expected to devote all their time and attention to serving the Lord. They should leave behind all other personal affairs, for when they accepted to go on the trip, they are accountable to the Lord and to those they are representing.

When the missionary and their mission partner are assigned to a specific mission area, they must remember that they are representing the Lord in this area and are responsible for obtaining God's direction in carrying out their assignment in blessing the people there.

When they have questions or concerns, their first source of help is the Father in heaven. Seek God's guidance through the Scriptures and personal revelation. Their companion and district and zone leaders are the next sources of support. They can help with everyday matters. For special needs, such as illness or confidential matters, talk with the mission leader.

They must strive to represent the Lord according to the highest standards of obedience and conduct. Missionaries must keep their words, thoughts, and actions in harmony with the message of His gospel. Righteous conduct will influence the effectiveness of a missionary and their personal salvation.

Their conduct also affects the trust and confidence of non-members, members, and other missionaries have in them. They must conduct themselves at all times in such a way that everyone who sees them will recognize them as representatives of Jesus Christ.

Language

Language is one of the most important key for any mission, and it is a powerful tool. It can simply be divided in two forms, and these are the things that comes out of the mouth and one's bodily actions.

When it comes to languages, some languages have intimate or familiar words used only in addressing family and very close friends. Other languages have forms of address that express great respect, such as words used only when speaking to those who are seen as higher ranking.

Missionaries should be conscious of how they speak because refined, dignified language will clearly identify them as a servant of the Lord, and when they are praying among the people, it is better to pray in the same language as everyone.

Since a word can have different meanings when it comes to different cultures, it would be best for the missionaries to understand the language and culture of the place they are visiting prior to their trip. They should avoid using slangs and inappropriate casual language, even in the presence of their friends or peers in the group

They should show respect to the leaders by not using their first names (preferably, to use their title), for the Bible tells us, "Do not let any unwholesome talk come out of your mouths, but only what is helpful for building others up according to their needs, that it may benefit those who listen" (Ephesians 4:29, NIV).

To sum it up missionaries must show respect for others by using appropriate language, which includes correct forms of the words.

Body language

Body language are gestures that are being made when speaking, when spoken to or when reacting to situation, such as movement in response to a comment, observation, one's thoughts, their emotions or experiences. This can be subtle or not so subtle.

It is advisable to get instructions from the local leaders who are working with the missionary ministry on how to respond, or which of our actions can be okay or offensive.

Question: Name a few more thing that a mission can do in order to be successful in their language.
Discussion:_____
_____
_____
_____

Appearance

Missionaries should maintain a high standard of modesty and appearance at all times while on a mission trip. Their clothing and action should not cause the host country to question the validity as to why they are there. Missionaries should never allow their appearance or their behavior to draw attention away from the message they are called to do. Their appearance is often the first message others receive, and it should support what comes out of the mouth.

Appropriate dress and grooming will help the missionary earn respect and trust, for the wearing of appropriate clothing, such as conservative, professional clothing, should be consistent with their calling, and they should be neat and clean.

Dress code

Modesty in dressing

As a Christian missionary, one must be modest in their dressing at all times. I say this because even though one would think that no one is watching how they dress, behave, and act, I can assure that God is watching.

When anyone looks at a Christian missionary in the field, they must see God or the Christlike manner in them, not see the inappropriate dress they are wearing. They should not wear clothing and things that can attract the flesh, the "human mind," or wear things that are out of the culture range. This statement may seem harsh to some, however, as a female going to spread the Gospel of Jesus Christ, I would not wear low V-neck clothing; see-through clothing, very short or tight-fitting clothing.

My attraction to the people would be the hope that I bring the great message of our Savior, not to allow human nature to take over to cause distraction in one's mind.

One might say that the missionary should resist making themselves a temptation. Yes, I utmost agree, however, my question to that statement would be, how many of us see something, and how many of us do not take a second look?

As the senior pastor of the church asked the congregation in one of his preaching, "What are you thinking?" In my case, my question would be what are they thinking about, or where are their imaginations leading them to when they look at my inappropriate dressing.

It is understood that we, as human beings, take the information gathered by our eyes and process it in our brains all the time, and standard visual processing is prone to distractions, which is why it can be so hard for us to pay attention to one thing while filtering out others.

According to Alexandra Reichenbach, from the University College of London, our brains have separate hardwired systems that visually track our bodies, even when we're not paying attention. This network triggers reactions even before the conscious brain has time to process them.

All I can say to this is prayer is the key, and it is better to focus on God.

QUESTION: Do you have any suggestions about dressing?
DISCUSSION: _____
_____
_____
_____

Hygiene

My grandmother always would say, "Cleanness is next to godliness." No one should smell a missionary coming! They should bathe daily and, if possible, use deodorant. With clothing on hand, they must make sure they are clean, mended, and wrinkle free. The individual should not look as if they just crawled out of bed!

Most importantly, they should make sure that their hands are clean at all times since there would be a lot of handshaking or hugs.

Another important aspect is to keep the mouth smelling fresh. It would be great to always keep a small bottle of mouthwash or some breath mints on hand.

Footwear

Footwear should be practical, comfortable, and able to walk in, preferably flat-soled shoes or shoes with low heels and proper shoes, depending on the weather.

Accessories

Jewelry and other accessories should be very simple and should not attract attention. They should be very inexpensive pieces.

Hair and makeup

It would be great for the hair to be well-groomed, and the makeup should not call attention to oneself.

Scheduling

When it comes to scheduling, it is best that at least 90 percent of the mission's schedule be prepared before departing for the mission trip. There should be effective coordination between the mission leader and the host country leaders, and since the missionaries are the visitors, it would be best to leave the time line setup to the host country.

In many cases, the pastors of the church take the responsibility to provide transportation, and because of this, sometimes, they may be late because they are the ones who may be driving. As in the case of South America, the pastors worked very closely with the missionaries.

They also work closely with the police and law in their village. They are depended upon to solve some petty situations, such as domestic arguments and small fights or when there are incidents that involve a child or suicide.

Cultural and recreational activities

Missionaries must remember that the host church is responsible for all activities. They are expected to work alongside them and take their instruction from them and, in most cases, since it is a short-term mission, evangelism plays an important role, and this brings awareness to the area that "church people' are in the area.

It allows the pastor to introduce the missionaries to the village. As the missionaries do so, they are reminded that they must stay with their companion during all activities. They must then stay in their area unless they receive permission to leave it.

Safety

Missionaries must make sure that their environment is safe. They must be observant. They must avoid activities that may cause injuries. Stay out of areas that can cause harm. They should avoid gathering in large groups of missionaries when they visit public places.

Entertainment

Missionaries are not on a short trip to be entertained; they are there to do the work of the Lord, and any form of entertainment should be to draw souls to Christ. These entertainments should not be lengthy. It should be things that are pleasing in the sight of God.

The missionary should be respectful at all times and always include the host nation when doing any type of entertainment.

Television, radio, movies, videos, DVDs, internet

Time is of the essence. It would be best to avoid television, radio, movies, videos, DVDs, or the internet and use them only when necessary or for educational purpose.

Getting involved is the key, so the missionary should use things such as headphones in their private moments. This item can be seen as a form of isolating oneself form those around, especially when among many people.

Music

It would not be a very good idea for the missionary to listen to music that would pull their thoughts away from their work. They should listen only to music that is consistent and would draw them close to Christ. This is a time to invite the Spirit, for the missionary to focus on the work at hand, and to direct their thoughts and feelings toward Jesus Christ. Or they should listen to music that the host country is listening to so as not to offend others.

Electronics, videos, and computer equipment

The missionary should not use unauthorized electronic or video equipment, especially for personal use, or while joining in with the host nation's activities. They are there to get involved and assist with the people in need.

Camera

The host could advise you on the appropriate use of cameras.

The missionary must try to refrain from using their camera while working with the people. They should get permission to take pictures with the people, and if they plan to or there is a desire to publish, make sure to get a written permission.

Reading materials

Missionaries must remember where they are at all times, and when it comes to reading, they should only read books, magazines, and other materials on information about the Word of God and showing how one can be a child of God.

Group activities

In the case of group activities, in order to encourage everyone, the missionary should take part in group activities when asked. This will allow the host country to see them as team players.

The law of chastity

A mission trip should not be a place for sexual activity. All missionaries, including the leaders, should remember the reason for their trip, and that is to draw souls to Christ!

With this in mind, they should, at all times, behave like Christ and are expected to obey strictly the law of chastity, and this is forbidding any sexual conduct of any kind outside of marriage only after marriage. These violations also include touching the private parts of another person, whether under or over clothing.

In some cultures, the missionary may end up with a criminal conduct charge or find themselves married to the person. If the victim is a minor, penalties can be severe, including imprisonment, and also, the missionary would not be able to leave the country. Understand that when it comes to false charges, the missionary would not be able to leave the country either.

Missionaries should never be without their partner that was assigned to them. They must not flirt or behave in a manner of leading someone on.

In some cultures, the chief or leaders of the host village will offer their children to the missionary. Just say, "NO THANK YOU." Again, remember the reason for the mission trip.

Relationship among missionaries

It is advisable for missionaries to partner with each other for their mission trip. They are there to support each other in all phases of the mission work, to help each other learn and grow, to strengthen each other in times of difficulty, to provide protection from physical danger, false charges, temptation, and to provide encouragement.

They are on the mission to preaching the gospel two by two, exercising the same as stated in the Bible. While on the trip, the missionaries should show love and respect to each other, look for the good in each companion, find ways to serve each other, work together in a spirit of unity, be able to study together, talk to each other, support each other, and pray with each other.

It is not respectful for the missionaries to criticize or condemn each other with anyone, especially the host country. They should remember that they must understand that they have the responsibility to protect each other.

Missionary leaders

When it comes to the missionary leaders, if their conduct appears to be inconsistent with the above standards, it would be best to discuss it with them immediately, for perception appears to be nine-tenths of the law sometimes, and this form of behavior can put the mission in jeopardy. It is not advisable to discuss this matter or seek advice from other missionaries.

For example, due to the lack of knowledge about Christianity, in some cultures, the people would try to incorporate their lifestyle with the Christian religion, and it is not *inappropriate* for the man of a household to have many wives, and because of this, some parents may want to offer their daughters to the missionary leader, regardless if he is married or not. As stated in the Law of Chastity, *"JUST SAY NO."*

Opposite sex

It is not advisable for the missionary to be alone with, flirt with, or associate in any other inappropriate way with anyone of the opposite sex. They must remember, in some countries, some individuals are seeking opportunities to get out of their situation.

The missionary should not telephone, write, e-mail, or accept calls or letters from anyone of the opposite sex living within or near mission boundaries, any boundaries for that matter.

For example, missionaries are seen as the provider to the host countries, and there are those who would try to get closer physically to them, and this behavior will cause disruption among the ministry. If not being careful, the objective of the mission may change form drawing souls to Christ to having relationships.

Counseling

Do not get involved with any form of counseling with the host country. If the host country leader invites the missionary to sit in a counseling session, it is best to decline politely, or if they insist, and the missionary accepts, it is advisable to just plainly shut up. Remember, cultures are different in many ways, and the missionary's advice may cause more harm than good. Missionaries are only there for a short period of time, and that period of time is not enough to understand the culture.

For example, I am a certified pastoral counselor only in the United States, and I may have the knowledge and degree to prove it, however, despite the fact that I was born in the country where I am on a mission, it does not give me the right to advise or even share my experience with those of a different culture. (In some countries, there are no equal rights when it comes to a husband and wife or a young woman wanting to leave home and live on their own prior to marriage.)

Children

Due to the increasing legal complexities, be extremely careful around children, Missionaries should bear in mind that if they are charged with inappropriate behavior, they will find themselves involved in a lengthy court case, and if found guilty, they could face a substantial jail sentence and church disciplinary action.

Missionaries should never be alone with a child, regardless of the age. They should always have someone accompanying them at all times, and they should avoid any behavior that could be misunderstood, misrepresentative, or even appear to be inappropriate.

Let the host country take care of their children's welfare, and make sure that there is always an adult present, and one important aspect: it is advisable to seek permission from an adult in wanting to give any form of gifts, such as candy, cakes, or crackers.

Communicating with those who surrender their life to Christ

Missionaries should share responsibility when working with new converts. They should work alongside the host pastor. With the permission of the host pastor, the missionary can occasionally write to the new converts, for an occasional note will encourage, reassure, and comfort them, to include rekindling the joy they felt at the time when they surrendered their life to Christ, and not forgetting to write them occasionally and encourage them to be faithful. (remembering not to communicate with the opposite sex.)

The missionary should use their church office and not their personal address on any correspondence when communicating. Use the mission office address as the return address on any correspondence with the converts.

Additional community service

While on mission, the missionary may see some other form of mission activity they would like to participate in. Prior to making any plans, the missionary should seek the permission and guidance of the ministry leader so that proper procedures can be met.

The missionary my ask to participate in servicing, building, or other activities. When asked by the host country, they must be mindful of what they are doing at all times; only share appropriate knowledge that can help.

Local laws and customs

While on the mission trip, all missionaries are subjected to the same punishment as the local people in the country they are visiting, especially if the missionary is a United States diplomat.

All missionaries must obey all laws of the country, to include making sure that their passport and visa requirements are up to date, traffic laws, driver's license requirements, border regulations and customs laws, respecting the culture, customs, traditions, religious beliefs and practices, and sacred sites in the area where they serve.

Always act in harmony with the highest standards of consideration and courtesy.

Always observe local customs of etiquette and the common practices of the culture.

Follow the host or hostess in the use of utensils, and chew food with a closed mouth; be thoughtful by not eating too much if food is in short supply.

Always express your thanks.

Never suggest that people immigrate to another country, even for work or schooling.

You should not become involved in adoptions.

Do not ask your family or people from your home area to sponsor or become involved in these activities.

Do not ask for or accept money or sponsorship from members or others in your mission area.

If you are serving in a country other than your own, you must return to your own country without delay at the end of your mission. A missionary's failure to return home can make it more difficult for the church to obtain visas for future missionaries.

Remember that you are recognized as a missionary even before you talk with people. Do not do anything that is inappropriate or offensive, such as chewing gum in public. Such practices take away from your image as a minister of Jesus Christ.

In many countries, placing flyers, pamphlets, or other materials in or on mailboxes or on the windshield of parked cars is a violation of local laws.

Finances

In many mission trips, especially short-term missions, the missionaries are responsible for financing their trip. They must be able to budget their money, be thrifty and wise in how to spend. They must limit how often they eat, especially at restaurants, including fast-food restaurants, and they should not give away monies regardless of the temptation, especially at the beginning of their trip.

Offerings

The missionaries are responsible for giving the host church a lump sum offering upon arrival and funds for transportation during their trip. This is to offset all expenses, for they are there to give, not to take. Their offering should not only be money but their time well spent in participating in constructive things that would benefit the host country.

Housing

The mission leader approves where all missionaries will stay during their trip. It is advisable for everyone to stay at one place. They will be partnered with one another when it comes to sleeping arrangements. If a husband and wife are there, they will be together; all others will partner with the same sex when it comes to sleeping arrangements.

Physical and temporal well-being

Transportation

The host church is responsible for making arrangements when it comes to the transportation while on the mission trip. All arrangements will be made prior to arrival in the country

Health

Each missionary is responsible for their own health. Prior to travelling, they must make sure that they have some form of medical insurance in case of emergency; if taking medication, they must make sure that they have a full supply and be mindful of what they are consuming.

Security

The missionary must be vigilant at all times. They must listen to and follow the promptings of the Spirit, which can warn them of danger.

- They must be sensitive to anything that is out of the ordinary, especially anyone who watches them closely or asks probing questions.
- Stay away from unsafe areas.
- Travel after dark only in lighted areas.
- Vary the routes you travel.

- Always be in the company of one of the host country representatives.
- Missionaries should avoid situations that could lead to confrontations. They should stay away from public demonstrations and locations. Note: if the host churches are going to a public demonstration, the missionary still needs to decline to participate.
- The missionary must be careful of what they say and write in public and in private.
- They should not make any remarks in reference to any type of political or cultural circumstances, especially in letters or e-mails.
- They should not become involved in political or commercial activities or in discussions or arguments on political or economic topics.
- Do not photograph any type of government buildings, including embassies, airports, military installations, and other city, state, or national buildings.
- Try not to take pictures of civil unrest or demonstrations, sacred objects or statues.
- Do not get involved in pranks or jokes about terrorism or terrorist acts.

MISSIONARY ASSIGNMENT

The mission ministry leader gives the lay members in the group the opportunity to minister, and they are sometimes placed in leadership positions. It should never be viewed in a way to obtain personal recognition or advancement in any form. It should be seen as an opportunity to serve God and serve others.

They will be assigned to a church or organization where they would spend their time for the duration of the mission. The missionaries will work alongside the church members and take directions from them and should always remember to be wise in what they are doing at all time and always remember that they are representing God in every aspect.

Ministering

A missionary leader must be an effective chief administrator in order to carry out the work of the Lord and the mission. Their eyes must always be on the ball, for they are responsible for the overall operation of the ministry, and must be able to work in any area of the ministry when needed. To be proactive is the key to the success of the mission.

The leaders will be placed in positions where they will be dealing with churched and unchurched individuals, when it comes to all arrangement that has to be made, so they must be prayed for all the time. Their responsibility is what is known as "cradle to the grave" or "beginning to the end."

The missionary leader must be effective in organization, making sure everything is in its place at all times. They must be able to coordinate and be able to be spontaneous and be a good motivator, able to lift, encourage, inspire and bless, not sometimes but always, not forgetting the practice of self-care.

They must be able to work with the most difficult person, who would constantly distract them from their work at hand. Their leadership skills must be of excellence, and they must maintain a high standard of leadership and righteousness. Excellence includes their ability to have a vision, setting the example for others to follow, being able to work with almost anyone, and can be relied upon.

Responsibility while on a mission trip

They must be able to inspire and support the team by setting a good example to follow; represent the mission by carrying out the plans for the mission; able to be an effective communicator since they would be dealing with various offices and individuals in various capacities; have the spirit of love, unity, obedience, and hard work; able to encourage other members of the team to live in the highest standard possible; helpful in assisting the members and local nationals to become powerful and fruitful; having the ability to correct the attitudes or behavior of other missionaries; able to teach and, most importantly, to always remember that their loyalty is first to the Lord than to the works for the Lord.

Meetings

The mission ministry leader is responsible for bringing all members together at least four times to coordinate mission trips prior to departure for the mission.

During the mission trip, the mission leader is responsible for bringing the host country and the missionaries together. This is where introductions will be made and assignments will be distributed.

If there are any questions to be asked, all missionaries are to go directly to the mission leader, not the host country leader.

Selling of goods

It is prohibited for missionaries to sell any type of items or goods and services while on a mission trip. They are there to give and serve the Lord, not to receive any form of investment. This includes selling of books that the missionaries may have written.

Making promises

As human beings, we tends to show compassion, and as missionaries, the empathy that we feel for others can put us in a predicament, when the number one golden rule is broken when preparing to end a mission trip, and that is making promises.

Missionaries are not to make promises to the host churches. It can cause severe problems when the missionary does not keep their promise, and because of this, there will be development of distrust. Also, the missionary must remember that they are not only representing themselves; they are representing their church and their ministry.

Note: sometimes, a host church leader will go to the missionary when the missionary leader is not around and ask for the missionary's personal things for themselves, such as watches, computers, phones, and other small items. It is still advisable to discourage them.

However, if the missionary decides to send any gifts or items upon returning, it would be respectful to let the mission leader know. For example, my mission partner and me decided to bless a local church with a few items, such as used clothing, school supplies, and Bibles. Prior to sending the items, we notified the mission leader what we were doing.

It is not advisable to make promises that one is not sure that they can keep.

INFORMATION CARD

Have a card with the following information, one must be given to the mission leader, one to leave at home, and one to keep in person:

- Missionary name
- The country where you are a citizen of (include passport number)
- Church or organization name
- Mission leaders' names
- Place of destination
- The position and responsibility
- The host information
- Purpose of the mission or a missionary for the purpose of ____
- Type of insurance, both medical and travel
- A copy of the passport
- Languages spoken
- Type of medications taken
- List of things allergic to
- Name of the person or persons you will be partnered with during the trip (preferably, partnering with the same sex)

HOST COUNTRY PERCEPTION

The host country churches always address every visiting missionary as a pastor or minister. They have a very high perception and expectation of the missionaries and would easily relinquish their position and place it at the missionary's feet (a sign of showing respect), and because of this, the missionary should explain immediately who they are and their position in order to avoid any type of embarrassment.

As stated before, a missionary can be a pastor, a minister, an elder, or any ordained position of the church and can also be a lay person. It is an identifier of the individual gift or calling.

Every missionary can do everything

The host country churches do not know a lot about foreign countries, and when the people hear that they will have visitors, there is this anticipation that they will be getting a lot of things, or there is that feeling that everything will be okay when the missionaries arrive. This is why, upon arrival, the missionary should *not* give the local people false hope in promising to save them.

Missionaries are rich

Coming from a third world country myself, when the people are told that missionaries will be arriving, the first thought that comes to mind is the gifts that we would receive when they come. One's imagination of someone flying on a plane to come and visit us was special and refreshing and gives a feeling of joy.

There is that perception that the missionary has a lot of money to come so far, and not forgetting, bringing gifts.

Will provide all that they ask

There is that hope that when the missionaries arrive, the people will get all that they ask for. This is due to the fact that when some missionaries return to their country, they will send items back to the churches.

Not all missionaries are in a position to do so, and this is an area where the mission leader must remind the local leader that the main objective of the missionary visit is to save souls.

Listen to the missionaries rather than their local pastor

In some countries, there is a very high regard for pastors, and the people of the country knows it. The pastor is considered as the advisor, the problem solver, the teacher, and in many areas, the pastor is the person that the people goes to prior to going to the law.

In some cases, the local people will turn to the missionaries when they did not get their way or did not agree with the end results of what their local leaders told them.

The missionaries should decline to give any sort of advice and politely recommend them back to their pastor, especially for domestic disputes.

ESTABLISHING A MISSION MINISTRY

Mission purpose

The purpose of an outreach ministry, locally and internationally, is to spread the gospel of Jesus Christ in order to draw souls to Christ, and this would be done through ministering the Word of God, teaching the Word of God, engaging the unchurched; empowering all those that the ministry come into contact with, inspiring those who give their lives to Christ, learning about the people in order to communicate effectively, listening to the needs of the people, and partnering with all those who would want to hear about Jesus Christ.

All of this must be done through excellence, integrity, accountability, innovation, and inclusiveness which includes the following: researching the community needs, finding out what type of outreach mission is required; conducting surveys to locate the demand of what is needed, finding out the state in which the ministry is to be established, work with other outreach ministries in the area to get a better understanding of outreach, building a team, evaluating the need of the outreach mission, recruiting members who would support and advance the goals of the ministry, establishing a social media presence, seeking out passionate volunteers, funding the ministry, draft a ministry plan, acquiring any necessary licenses or permits, starting a fund drive, applying for grants, getting a tax exempt status, incorporating the ministry, getting an employer identification number, completing a nonprofit application if necessary, and apply for a local tax exemption.

Reason for the outreach mission

When we look at the decline in church attendance, both in North America and internationally, we can see that there is a need for outreach ministries. There is a need for laborers to be in the fields so that the Word of God can be spread rapidly and quickly in order for many people to come to Christ and be saved, so that they can experience the wonderful love of Jesus Christ.

As the Bible tells us many times, the harvest is plentiful, and the laborers are few. This is shown in Matthew 28:19, Matthew 9:38, Matthew 20:1, Luke 10:2, John 4:35, James 5:4, and Mark 16:15.

> Therefore go and make disciples of all nations, baptizing them in the name of the Father and of the Son and of the Holy Spirit. (Matt. 28:19, NIV)

The Parable of the Workers in the Vineyard:

> For the kingdom of heaven is like a landowner who went out early in the morning to hire workers for his vineyard. (Matt. 20:1, NIV)

> He told them, "The harvest is plentiful, but the workers are few. Ask the Lord of the har-

> vest, therefore, to send out workers into his harvest field." (Luke 10:2, NIV)
>
> Don't you have a saying, "It's still four months until harvest"? I tell you, open your eyes and look at the fields! They are ripe for harvest. (John 4:35, NIV)
>
> Look! The wages you failed to pay the workers who mowed your fields are crying out against you. The cries of the harvesters have reached the ears of the Lord Almighty. (James 5:4, NIV)
>
> He said to them, "Go into all the world and preach the gospel to all creation." (Mark 16:15, NIV)

The increase in laborers would be beneficial to the outreach mission because they would be able to reach many people so that they can tell them about the gospel of Jesus Christ, especially those who have turned away from Christ, the unchurched, and those who call themselves "non-Christians," which are increasing in our environment according to authors David Kinnaman and Gabe Lyons.

Decrease in church attendance

There is a decrease in church attendance, not only in North America, but it appears that this is internationally also, especially in the Christianity committee.

In the African Continent, it is understood that the population is predominately Muslim, and it is only 17 percent

Christian, and even though many missionaries are traveling there to spread the Gospel, there seems to be a decrease in saving souls, rather than an increase.

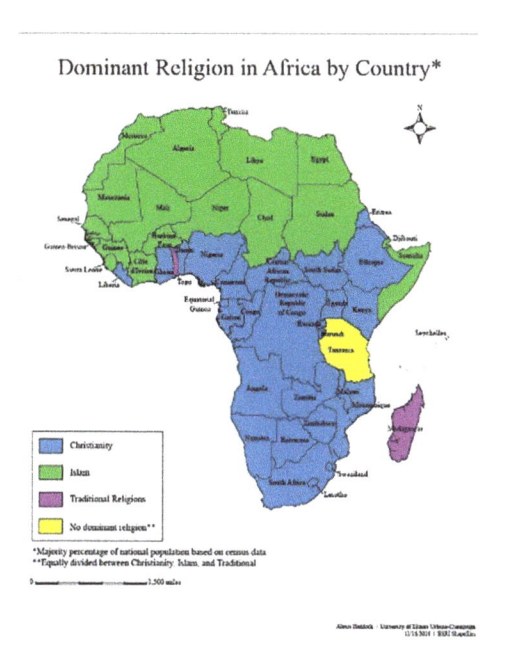

Dominant Religion in Africa by Country*

In case of the Christians who are located in South America, in such a countries as Guyana, where I was born, there is a decrease in church attendance. The problem is how and what to do to show the population that there is a God, and that He sent His son to die on the cross for our sins.

Outreach Mission Ministry will always be in an evangelism, outreach, and mission mode all the time, for the common denominator of all three would be to draw souls to Christ.

As Christians go beyond the four walls of the church, they are not only going to outreach; they are first evangelizing because when they meet someone, they will be in an evangelizing mode and have the opportunity to invite those that responded to church. On the other hand, if they cannot attend church and are willing to hear the Word of God, they are being met where they are, and this is where the outreach mode comes into mind. And in some cases, those we are reaching out to may need a snack or a bottle of water, and this is a form of mission.

I learned that the term outreach is stated in the Bible.

> Preach the word; be prepared in season and out of season; correct, rebuke and encourage with great patience and careful instruction. (2 Tim. 4:2, NIV)

> Therefore go and make disciples of all nations, baptizing them in the name of the Father and of the Son and of the Holy Spirit, and teaching them to obey everything I have commanded you. And admittedly I am with you always, to the very end of the age. (Matt. 28:19–20, NIV)

PREPARATION FOR MISSION

The missionaries must be involved in training. They must have the ability to teach, inspire and instill in people the desire to live a Christlike lifestyle, and have faith and believe that there is a true and living God, despite the fact that they do not physically see Him.

The missionary must be able to work cooperatively with others of mutual purpose in accomplishing the task of saving souls, however, the first task at hand would be after God has granted them the vision, which they have accepted, and come to the understanding that this is what they want to do.

Prior to announcing to anyone that an individual would like to get involved with outreach mission because God has called them to do so, they must examine themselves to see if they have the burden for this type of ministry and should ask themselves many questions, such as the following:

- Is it a vision from God, or is it something they want to do?
- Is it something that they are ready to commit to doing either short term or long term?
- Are they someone who can work with others?
- Are they someone that is trainable?
- Are they equipped to establish the ministry?
- Are they someone who is adaptable with guidelines?
- Are they someone who can make sacrifices?

- Are they someone who can have the desire to be Christlike always?
- Are they willing to take responsibility?

If all of these answers are yes, then the next thing to decide is when it would be the right time to commit to establishing the outreach ministry, and that individual must always pray and ask God for guidance and making sure that they are seeking answers from God and not man.

Establishing an outreach mission, especially international outreach, is not as easy as one would believe. It includes a lot of planning and patience. As one surrenders their life to Christ, He—God—blesses them with spiritual calling so that they can do His works to draw souls to Him.

That individual must be prepared to do God's work all the time, and some spiritual gifts will be added on, not only to them but to other ministry members, which would be directly related to outreach mission, and these gifts and calling are of great practical value which would have many benefits to the believers in order for them to spread the Gospel.

This is where the outreach mission members would go beyond the four walls of the church, reaching lost souls where they are and doing the will of God by showing people that there is a God, and God loves everyone. And this is one of the reasons why God sent His Son to die on the cross to save His children and forgive them of their sins.

When someone received the vision or thirst for God to spread the Gospel outside the church, they must also not move in haste but must seek God's guidance in every area so that they will not reach disaster especially when it comes to any Christian outreach.

Those who God has given that vision to spread the Gospel must have received Christ as their personal savior. They must have the willingness to accept their assignment and must examine themselves to make sure that they have a Christlike character. And that is stated in 2 Timothy 3, since they would be a leader who is representing God.

> But mark this: There will be terrible times in the last days. People will be lovers of themselves, lovers of money, boastful, proud, abusive, disobedient to their parents, ungrateful, unholy, without love, unforgiving, slanderous, without self-control, brutal, not lovers of the good, treacherous, rash, conceited, lovers of pleasure rather than lovers of God—having a form of godliness but denying its power. Have nothing to do with such people. They are the kind who worm their way into homes and gain control over gullible women, who are loaded down with sins and are swayed by all kinds of evil desires, always learning but never able to come to a knowledge of the truth. Just as Jannes and Jambres opposed Moses, so also these teachers oppose the truth. They are men of depraved minds, who, as far as the faith is concerned, are rejected. But they will not get very far because, as in the case of those men, their folly will be clear to everyone. You, however, know all about my teaching, my way of life, my purpose, faith, patience, love, endurance, persecutions, sufferings—what kinds of things happened to me in Antioch, Iconium and Lystra, the persecutions I endured. Yet the Lord rescued me from all of them. In fact, everyone who wants

to live a godly life in Christ Jesus will be persecuted, while evildoers and impostors will go from bad to worse, deceiving and being deceived. But as for you, continue in what you have learned and have become convinced of, because you know those from whom you learned it, and how from infancy you have known the Holy Scriptures, which are able to make you wise for salvation through faith in Christ Jesus. All Scripture is God-breathed and is useful for teaching, rebuking, correcting and training in righteousness, so that the servant of God may be thoroughly equipped for every good work. (2 Timothy 3)

These characters include being loving and compassionate, honest and accountable, loyal, humble. They must be individuals of confidence; must have the characteristic of convictions; must be someone of commitment, someone of compassion, communication, humility, and show tenderness, passion, and discipline. They must be able to recognize the value in other people, so they continually invest in others. They share information with those in the organization, has above average character, uses their influence for the good of others, is skillful and competent, not afraid for others to succeed even higher than their success, serves others expecting nothing in return, continues to learn, remains accessible, approachable and accountable to others, and is a visionary who thinks for the organization beyond today.

In addition, they must have genuine enthusiasm and be great listeners. Their identity is not their vocation, and they must be intentional about personal witnessing. They have the unconditional love for Christ. They have a gentle spirit, and they persevere and must pray about what God is telling them to do. And as they begin to plan, they must create a list and continue to add information to their list continually.

The first attempt is to understand the type of mission, the priorities, the areas of work, and the type of activities needed—brainstorming, identifying, assessing, drafting, and then evaluating. In this case, a list must be made to establish the steps needed to be taken.

The steps to establish an international ministry

Creating a mission statement

When creating a mission statement, it must be brief and to the point, and it must show every area of the international ministry's mission. It must also grab the attention of those who read it or those who may want to participate. When completed, when one reads it, they must decide the intent of the ministry and why the department is important.

Establishing a committee

This is known as a board of directors or a ministry, which would include at least about four to six members to include a ministry leader, a coordinator, a financial director, a logistics operator, an administrator, and a communications personnel. Each job must have a job description, and each member must sign it. It would be great if there are more people.

Each job description must be tailored to the area where the mission would be (except the pastor), the ministering, and praying, and it is understood that a ministry cannot be established by oneself. They will need a team of people to help with networking, organizing, gathering, and training those who respond to the invitation to be a part of a new ministry, and this team should come from a set of enthusiastic people.

There should be a group of people who share the ministry leader's conviction that this ministry should exist. They must be willing to give sacrificially of their time, talents, and treasures to ensure that this church is a success. In most cases, they will be among the new people who want to know God.

It would be encouraged for the leader to look to God or discern who they choose to launch the ministry. They should pay attention to their motivation, health, and skill sets as they anticipate the future needs of their new church. The launch team should consist primarily of spiritual "worker bees"—these are people with deep faith and strong leadership skills willing to work tirelessly to plant this church. They should be team players who are committed to embracing and executing God's vision of this new ministry as expressed through the ministry leader's response to points of resistance as a united front.

This new ministry team ideally will also bring valuable skill sets to the side, such as someone who is a graphic or web designer and could help the ministry with their technological needs. Someone may be a business person in the community that can help with networking with outstanding leaders. It could be someone who is a member of the local government board and can introduce the ministry leader to other councils members or a member of a parent-teacher association where the ministry leader can be presented to parents and teachers. It could also be someone who is a real estate agent and can help you meet new people who move into your community.

The new ministry team should be willing to draw on their skills, networks, and social connections to get people involved with the new ministry, and also, the people living in your mission field will tell you what kind of outreach is right for the neighborhood. And the ministry leader must always remember that their job is to listen, pray, discern and, together, build the ministry God is calling them into.

Registering the name

When choosing a name for the mission, it would be better to come up with about three different names. This is to avoid duplication, and make sure that there is no other organization with the same name. The ministry leader must research every avenue to make sure before contacting the state in which they want to register the ministry.

When contacting the Department of Revenue Bureau for registration of the ministry, the registrar will complete another research in their database system to make sure there is no duplication in their data and if there are no other names. The clerk would register the name that the ministry leader submitted, and in turn, the clerk would send the ministry leader a form with instruction, with a request for a certain amount of fee which must be paid.

The payment would be either a bank check, money order, or personal check. When this is done, the ministry will receive a document with a number and a certificate. This signifies that no one is authorized to use that name because it belongs to the department, and from this point, all correspondence for the ministry will have that name.

After registering the ministry, the name is completed, and the department will be required to advertise the new name in a newspaper of general circulation in the county in which your business will be located. They can also identify the publication by contacting the county courthouse or county bar association.

Filing an Article of Incorporation

This document protects the ministry and the offices from legal liabilities that occur in the department. It is a requirement by the state. It would be important for the ministry leader to contact the state office so that this can be adequately done.

Corporation is the most complex form of business organization to create, primarily because of the paperwork required to establish a corporation. Business activities are restricted to those listed in the corporate charter. However, most corporations define business activities in broad terms in the charter. There are two types of corporations in Pennsylvania: C corporations and S corporations. The income and losses of each are determined using different rules.

While C corporations follow federal income tax rules for determining income with some adjustments, S corporations must use PA personal income tax rules for determining income, as well as book income, for determining capital stock/foreign franchise tax. Advantages of a corporation structure include the limitation of liability to the amounts owners have contributed to shares of stock and the fact that a corporation's continuity is unaffected by the death of or transfer of shares by any owner.

Disadvantages include extensive record keeping, close regulation, and double taxation, since profits are taxed at the corporate level, and dividends paid to owners are taxed at the individual level.

In forming a corporation, prospective shareholders transfer money and property for the corporation's capital stock. Remember that the articles of incorporation and a docketing statement must be filed with the Corporation Bureau of the Department of State., and upon completion, the ministry leader will have to send the document to the Internal Revenue with the proper amount of payment.

This process takes from three to six months to process, so it would be wise to make sure that it is done correctly. If not, it will take up to about two years and, in some cases, additional fees are required.

Establishing a ministry by law

Since this is a legal document also, and it governs the ministry, it would be better to have it legally done for it is a binding document that must be completed and approved by all the members in the department. This document is the set of rules that are established and reinforced by the ministry. It includes all job description and responsibilities that each ministry members must comply with, making sure that a copy of the job description must be signed by each appointed members, with the intent of fulfilling all.

Applying for an Employer Identification Number (EIN)

Employer identification numbers are used to identify the tax accounts of employers, sole proprietors, corporations, partnerships, estates, trusts, and other entities. This is a document that must be filled out and filed by the Ministry to the Internal Review. Upon approval, the Internal Review would send a report with the appropriate number which would be used to open a bank account or proof that a company exists.

Filing for tax exemption status with the Internal Revenue Service

These are documents in the form formats and must be completed and submitted to the IRS with a fee. It is better to contact the IRS so that the correct form can be completed.

When this is approved, it opens the door for the ministry to accept donations, pay for a product without paying the tax, and have the opportunity to operate in the same category with churches and other nonprofit organizations.

Opening a bank account

To open a bank account, it would be considered a business account. With the document that the internal revenue provides, along with the name of the ministry leader, the officers, and their credentials, the bank account can be open. Aside from this, it would be advisable to establish a separate business bank account, and the ministry will find it very helpful to open a bank account for sales tax you collect from customers or withholding taxes deducted from employees' compensation.

When this is done, the organization is established, but there is more work to be done. There is the preparation of articles which provides at least ten steps. It offers specific steps and instructions for the ministry leader to follow, and it is being used as a textbook of instructions.

It is very important to explain the project plan to the ministry. There must be step-by-step procedures so that it can be understood. It must provide the direction from beginning to end to include the project plan, showing short range and long range, teaching the importance of the program, project plan showing the baselines which are known as performance measures

The baselines, which are the performance measures, must show the scope of the ministry, the extent to which the department must work with, such as showing all the things the department will do, and every instruction must be written down and placed in a procedure binder.

Defining the roles and responsibilities of each officer and member

The ministry leader will be responsible for the entire project and takes responsibility as seen.

The coordinator is responsible for making all arrangements and makes sure every aspect of ministry is organized and is working well.

The starting date

This will begin when all points of the department are completed, approved, to include financial assistance and grants. It will be best to have a meeting to explain the status of the ministry for it is good to have open communication.

Some of the matters that can be discussed are:

* *Ministry vision.* Even though it is the ministry leader who received the vision to establish a ministry, when coming together, other members of the team can submit their input.
* *Project vision.* This has a wide range. The main project will be to draw souls to Christ beyond the four walls of the church. There should be additional inputs on how this will be done and what will be the requirements.
* *Roles and responsibilities.* There would be many roles, and each individual should be buried on their responsibility, making sure of what is required of them.
* *Team building.* Working together always and communicating always would be effective in making the ministry a success.
* *Team committees.* Some members will be working in teams so that they may be able to coordinate among each other.

* *How to make wise decisions.* This will be done by seeking God's guidance and following rules that are laid out.
* *Ground rules to follow.* There are many requirements that need to be followed, especially when travelling to a different country.
* *What is the expectation.* To see success in what is to be done with limited danger.
* *Development of a scope statement.* This is where each activity must be expressed in detail, and these are the business needs and business problem.
* *Project objectives.* This include what will occur with the ministry to solve the ministry business problems, the benefits of completing the ministry as well as the ministry justification.
* *Ministry scope.* This will show what projects will be kept and what will be excluded for the ministry project, especially internationally.
* *Key store milestone.* This will be to identify the range of the ministry to show at what point to stop.
* *Developing a scope baseline.* This can be done when the ministry decides what points they will do in supporting.
* *Develop the schedule and cost baselines.*
* *Create a baseline management plan.*
* *Develop the staffing plan*: There are many areas to be worked on which will overlap with each other.
* *Analyze projects quality and risks*: Each action must be reviewed and must be communicated effectively with everyone involved. This is very important in all aspects when planning a ministry.

RESEARCHING INFORMATION

In the preparation of and international plan, the ministry leader will coordinate with the international country when the decision is made to go internationally to spread the gospel. The coordinator of the outreach ministry must have already researched and found a country to see if they are safe for receiving missionaries. It is best to complete an intense research on countries that are safe, and this can be done mostly with the United States Department website.

The website will show the facts of the country, and these are the population, the name of the various cities, the government department and their addresses and phone numbers, in the event that someone would want to contact them, and many other information of the country.

In the case of religion and culture, it would be better the contact the country itself to get an accurate and updated response such as in the case of Guyana, South America. Contact the country's foreign affairs department through a phone call to get the correct address to write a letter of request for a letter of intent.

In the letter, the ministry leader will explain that there is a missionary ministry located in the United States who would like to visit their country to share the gospel with their citizens and would like their permission to enter the country.

The ministry may want to find out the following:

- what type of seasons the country has
- the type clothing that are needed
- when is the best time to travel
- how many languages and types of cultures
- type of currencies
- type of people
- are the people receptive to strangers?
- type of living environment
- type of seasons
- medical situation
- the needs of the people
- political environment
- security
- where can a meeting be held
- cost of supplies
- reliable leaders

The ministry must also seek permission to visit one of the villages who speaks English and has one type of culture. The reason for this is because when traveling to a country for the first time, it is better to move slowly and become familiar with the history of the country, their likes and dislikes, along with the various cultures, languages, and procedures of greeting. They must also request a welcome packet be sent to the ministry with a point of contact.

As in the case of a country such as Guyana, there are those who speak one language and one religion, one tongue and two cultures or two worlds, and there are also six nations living together, with three dominant religions such as Hindu, Muslim, and Christian. They speak English, and choosing an area to spread would not be difficult: When looking at the chart below, one can see the percentage of those who are Christians.

Religions - Guyana

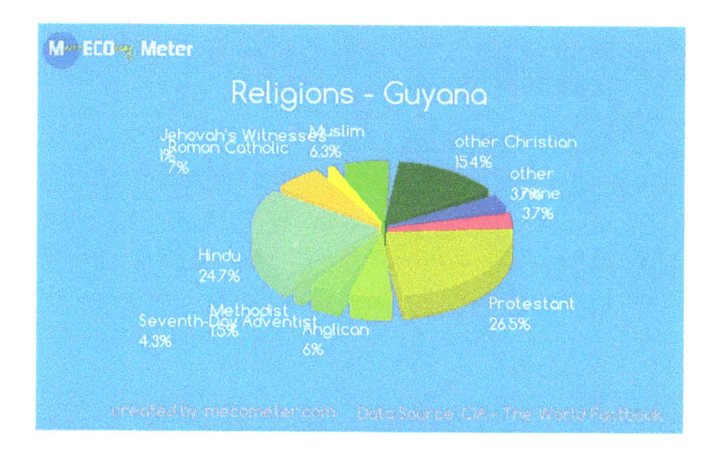

(Pie chart showing: Jehovah's Witnesses, Muslim 6.3%, Roman Catholic 7%, other Christian 15.4%, other 3.7%, none 3.7%, Protestant 26.5%, Anglican 6%, Methodist 1.5%, Seventh-Day Adventist 4.3%, Hindu 24.7%)

As it is said in the Bible, the harvest is plentiful, and the laborers are few, so we are going to make more laborers as we join the other laborers to spread God's word. "Then He said to his disciples, 'The harvest is plentiful, but the workers are few'" (Matthew 9:38)

The ministry must also research on their own about the country and get acquainted of the location of the country, and they must also contact their foreign office to see if it is safe to travel to that country and the requirements, including the type of currencies, travel insurances, hours to visit, cost to fly, if visa is required, and how much time it will take to receive, and to ask if there are forms that have to be filled out prior to traveling.

Other important research would include finding out if the countries accepts missionaries, and if there are other missionaries in the country and where they are located. Also, the ministry must understand that countries who receive missionaries show that there is always a need, and it is not good to visit without taking some items that are needed for those in need.

These things are clothing, food, and other miscellaneous small items that are essential. The people will be more apt to listening, for no one listens to what one has to say if they are hungry. With this is in mind, reaching out to other ministries who are physically in the country or who visited prior would be great to get advice on what to do and what not to do.

They can also get information on the types of items to take, get to understand the culture in the form of what to do and what to expect, finding out modes of transportations, the types of weather such as when is the best time to travel to the country, the type of food that are consumed, and find out about the type of illness in the areas, to include local crime rates, and the requirement to travel.

A phone should be set as a direct point of contact. This phone number must be listed in all communication and all letters, and an email should be established with a proper letterhead return address, and all of this is created while the development of the ministry are in.

Prior to getting involved in any ministry, it is wise to get training, and the committed leaders of the ministry should begin to get training and refresher training on every aspect so that they can train the rest of the ministry members, especially when it comes to how to operate internationally.

The types of training and courses are: understanding how to communicate, choosing the right time and place, making sure there is a clear understanding of what is being said, knowing how to convey information so that both sides can understand especially in different cultures, engaging in proper listening, understanding nonverbal communication, managing stress in body movement, asserting oneself in a respectful manner, always staying in focus, and being mindful of inconsistent body language, thereby understanding what is positive or negative body language. The ministry member must also be able to open an intimate conversation, remove distractions while communicating, and organize and clarify ideas in their mind when needed. They must know how to evangelize and how to tell people about who God is, how to be able to work among peers and subordinates under a culture that is different in every area, and they must have some form of hands-on training. That is why it would be better to get involved with a few outreach missions in the community before branching out internationally. This experience would give them the boldness to interact with anyone to be able to talk about Jesus Christ freely and openly pray to God. The training must be on:

- why do personal evangelism,
- sources of prospects,
- setting up the study,
- what to say,
- conducting the study,
- persuasion,
- closing the study,
- handling objections and answering questions,
- able to answer questions on salvation, and
- have knowledge on denomination and world religions.

In this case, one will have to identify who are the audience of the outreach. If it is preaching in the street, the ministry will get the experience on how to plan for this. They will get to practice speaking in public on their own, and they must make sure that prior to going in the street, they must have security and all other resources in order to preach the gospel, to press the doctrine, such as a microphone, flyers to give out, and also have at least two or more people in the community that is formed. They must make sure that they notify the local police, depending on the street they will be outreaching.

If going to a nursing home, make sure to submit a letter to their office to get permission, and make sure an approval is given in writing and also that the ministry schedule and the ministry date are in one accord. Remember, at some places, another ministry may want to take a few items to give away to attract the people in the community so that they may need want to stop and listen to the Word of God. This is where the ministry is including missions in the outreach; they're not only preaching the gospel but is providing a need

In this case, the supplies that are given out should either be purchased by the church, donated by church members, reaching out to the stores for assistance, and finding various honorable ways to get funds to buy items, or ask for the things to be donated. At this point, there must be prepared plans to get the details before setting a date to minister.

In the case of when hot food is needed, there must be coordination with other ministries in advance, ministries such as hospitality, who would be responsible for preparing the meals in a manner to suit those who are in need, also, a prayer ministry who is responsible for praying for those who request special prayer.

To the place that this project would be done, a letter of permission must be sent out, a schedule must be prepared in advance, and the program includes preaching the gospel, praise and worship, prayer, and ministering and serving. Coordination will be done for these, and at the project, there must be accountability such as how many guests arrived, how many requested prayers, how many surrendered their life to Christ.

When serving hot meals, it would be advisable to find out about the type of meals needed, the total amount of guests, find out if children are included, and make sure all needs are met. The ministry will learn not to put themselves in harm's way. This can be done simply by following all the rules that apply to where they are go to perform outreach.

They must be able to work together as a team, which is very important for success. It would allow the ministry to be able to exchange ideas, work on big projects and follow through with goals that were established. We learn that a good team is never just a coincidence. This requires a lot of work from both the ministry leader and its members, which requires open communication, clear vision, and clear ministry activity roles, and they will learn how to communicate effectively and being able to spread the gospel.

A financial plan must be made. The ministry must begin by defining their financial goals, both short term and long term, and these goals will become the driving force of their financial plan, for the main purpose of financial planning is to allow the ministry to influence their own future by thinking and acting in advance. It is to help the ministry to achieve their goals through proper management of their finances. It is the process of asking questions to ensure that the ministry can manage their risk against unexpected events.

A financial plan is mainly a formal process of developing a road map of financial goals while taking into consideration the ministry assets, liabilities, and credit standing. It is also a comprehensive overview of the ministry financial standing and goals as long as the ministry is operational.

This plan must include everything that one can think of that can make the ministry a success. As in the case locally, the department must begin by including the cost for supplies, administration, pieces of equipment, cost to travel, the cost for the need to hand out to the people, and communication lines.

Financial plan example

Profit & Loss	April	May	June	July	August	September	October	November	December	January	February	March
Revenues												
No of Units Sold	1200	1500	1800	2200	2700	2500	2300	3000	3400	3700	4000	4000
Price per unit	100	100	100	100	100	100	100	100	100	100	100	100
Total Revenues	120000	150000	180000	220000	270000	250000	230000	300000	340000	370000	400000	40000
Variable Expenses												
No of Units	1200	1500	1800	2200	2700	2500	2300	3000	3400	3700	4000	4000
Variable Cost per Unit	25	25	25	27	27	27	27	27	27	28	28	28
Total Variable Cost	30000	37500	45000	59400	72900	67500	62100	81000	91800	103600	112000	112000
Fixed Expenses												
Manpower	34500	34500	34500	34500	34500	34500	34500	34500	34500	34500	34500	34500
Marketing	65000	65000	65000	65000	80000	80000	80000	80000	45000	40000	40000	35000
Travel	3000	3000	3000	3000	3000	3000	3000	3000	3000	3000	3000	3000
Telephone	1000	1000	1000	1000	1000	1000	1000	1000	1000	1000	1000	1000
Rent	20000	20000	20000	20000	20000	20000	20000	20000	20000	20000	20000	20000
Capital Costs	0	0	0	0	0	0	0	0	0	0	0	0
Miscellaneous	3000	3000	3000	3000	3000	3000	3000	3000	3000	3000	3000	3000
Total Expenses	156500	164000	171500	185900	199400	194000	203600	222500	198300	205100	213500	208500
Profit Before Tax	-36500	-14000	8500	34100	70600	56000	26400	77500	141700	164900	186500	191500
Tax @ 30%												
Profit After Tax					79240	39200	18480	54250	99190	115430	129920	134050

If the ministry leader has the support of a church, the ministry leader must first meet with the board of the church to tell them of their intention. They would let them know of the vision by writing a formal letter. They must send this letter to the board of the church. The message must state that the individual would like to establish an outreach mission and is asking permission to build one; they must explain that it was their calling and state how the ministry would benefit the church.

If the church responds with a positive light, they may volunteer to assist totally or halfway; either way; it would be a blessing because there is a backing. The church may have a stipulation for the ministry to comply, and upon hearing this, there is the decision to name the ministry.

They will not need an added phone line because they will be able to use the church address and phone, also, they may not have to apply for financial assistance or grants; however, they will have to perform all the other function that is mentioned, including coordinating and communicating with those outside the church to get things done.

The ministry will not have to complete the following steps also:

- Applying for a nonprofit, which may need a 501(c)(3)
- Send name to the state to register the name
- Receive approval from the state
- Open a bank account using the number on the document that is given by the state
- Receive an EIN from the Bank
- Begin writing letters for donation
- Begin writing request for grants

The ministry where the church does not support would be encouraged to solicit for financial assistance. When it comes to financial assistance to operate the ministry, since grants take a long time to process, it would be great to solicit donation from the community, other churches, friends and other small business. This is done by reaching out to everyone by writing letters to them explaining the ministry intent and plans. Sometimes, they may want to see proof of the ministry plan and budget and, sometimes, goes to the extent of asking for proof that there is an application process for nonprofit because if they donate monies to establish the ministry, it is a guarantee to some of them especially the small business.

They may want to use that information for their internal revenue needs. These monies can be used as a startup for the ministry, such as paying for legal assistance for writing up plans, creating the ministry budget plan, and completing all other required applications, to include administration fees and completing grants applications.

In reference to applying for grants, it is advisable to apply for grants as early as possible because the processing time can take more than a year. The ministry must research and become acquainted with the type of grants that are available and which suit the needs of the outreach mission ministry. The ministry must always be on the lookout for new grants because there are always new grants available weekly in the city.

The ministry should obtain a grant writer that have the knowledge of outreach ministries because they would be familiar in writing the grants and making sure that it is written in detail, thoroughly and in a timely manner, and when the grants are approved, understand that the work is just beginning for there would be many more information to submit requested by those who granted the approval.

To understand the processing of grants, some of the things that are advisable first, to start preparing grant applications early. This will allow plenty of time to get all required information to be submitted long before the submission deadline.

Always follow the Notice of Funding Opportunity in detail and prepare all the requested information in order. When preparing, keep your audience in mind. Please do not assume that the reviewers are familiar with your ministry. Be brief, clear, and concise by providing accurate and honest information, to include accounts of problem and difficult situations and explain in detail honestly and make sure to add all attachments.

Be organized and logical, making sure the thought process is clear and workable and fits the ministry goals. Show evidence of fiscal table and accurate fiscal management. This demonstrates the strength and ability of the ministry. There are many technical details, so make sure they are written clearly. Only use attachments that are required. If there are electronic applications, proofread and review before submitting. Make sure all information is submitted at the same time.

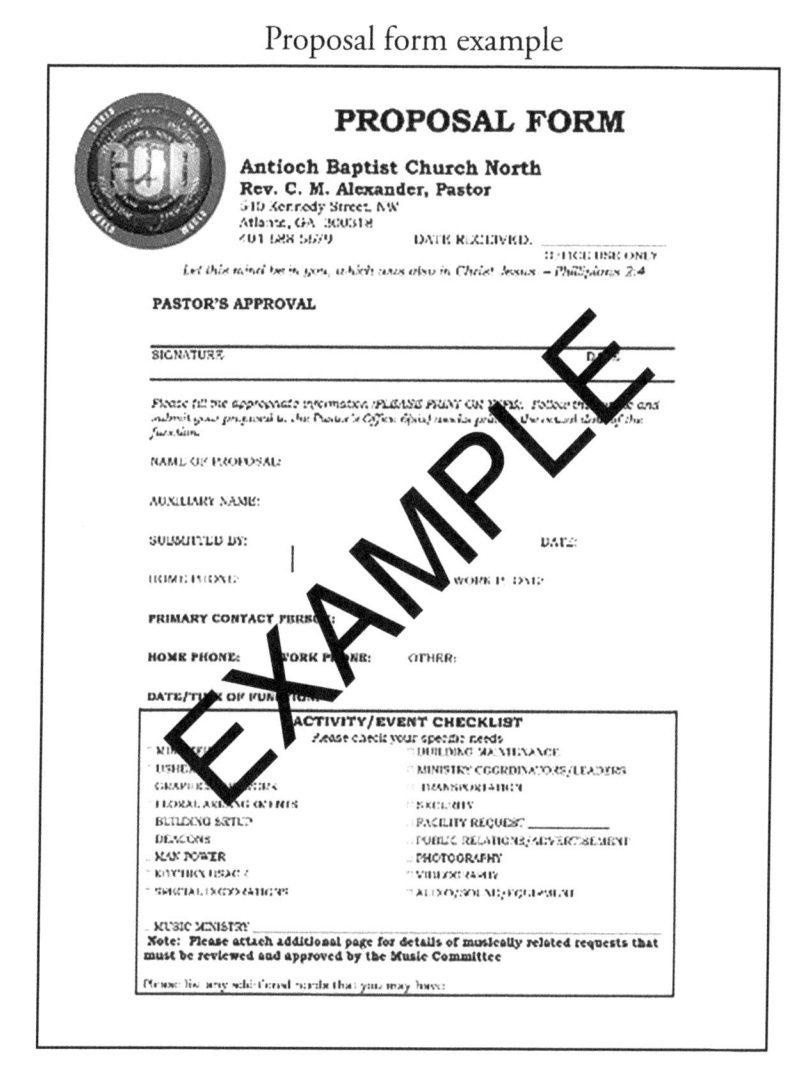

Proposal form example

PROPOSAL FORM

Antioch Baptist Church North
Rev. C. M. Alexander, Pastor

(EXAMPLE)

This project is to establish an outreach ministry locally and internationally. It is to capture the basic steps in doing so. When it comes to establishing an outreach ministry, it involves many parts, especially when dealing internationally. Many people are in involved in various stages in order to make it a success.

There are short- and long-term goals. Some steps to establishing would overlap each other. Not everyone the ministry leader would be interacting with has surrendered their life to Christ, and there would be times when they would have to be patient and seek guidance to get things done, and the ministry leader must remember that the passion that they have for the ministry to begin may not be the same as the rest of the ministry member, so they will all have to stand firm in their decision and keep track of everything that needs to be done.

When all plans are completed, and the outreach ministry is satisfied, that is when the ministry will become operational. They are then creating an environment that will foster the love of Christ.

We learned that it is important to spread the Gospel because this is what the Lord wants us to do, and every Christian should have a thirst in them to spread the Gospel regardless of where they are. They should have that evangelism mode in them all the time and want to reach people where they are to tell about Jesus and not be ashamed to do so.

Outreach ministry members must be able to create an environment of being comfortable when talking about God. They should be in a place within themselves where they do not feel judged but feel accountable, and they must use the Holy Spirit always, and developing a successful plan is the first step.

ESTABLISHING A BUSINESS CHECKLIST

Checklist for business start-up:

- Entrepreneurial assistance
- Sole proprietorships
- Partnership
- Limit Liability companies
- Corporations
- State S corporations
- Identifications numbers
- Registering for PA Tax Accounts
- Registrations required with other agencies
- Fictitious name
- Common sense about your business
- Business expenses
- Depreciation
- Record keeping
- Supporting documents
- Bookkeeping systems
- How long to keep records
- State you are in tax enforcement
- Taxable sales
- Tax year
- Personal income tax
- Employer withholding

- Taxpayer assistance
- The state tax credits
- Revenue district offices

Letter of registration example

Account cycle for the ministry example

Accounting Cycle diagram with steps: Collect Source Documents → Verify Source Documents → Analyze Transactions → Journalize Transactions → Post to Ledger → Prepare Trial Balance → Prepare Worksheet → Prepare Financial Statements (EXAMPLE)

Ministry budget example
Proposed church planting budget
Worksheet for Fiscal Year 20__

Expenses

Application Fee to register Ministry Name	$1000.00
Article Fees	$800.00
Supplies	$500.00
Equipment	$2000.00
Phone Fee	$200.00
Building Fee	$1500.00
Utilities Fees	$500.00

Request for donation example

MISSIONARY ONBOARD!

Request for grants example, depending on the state location

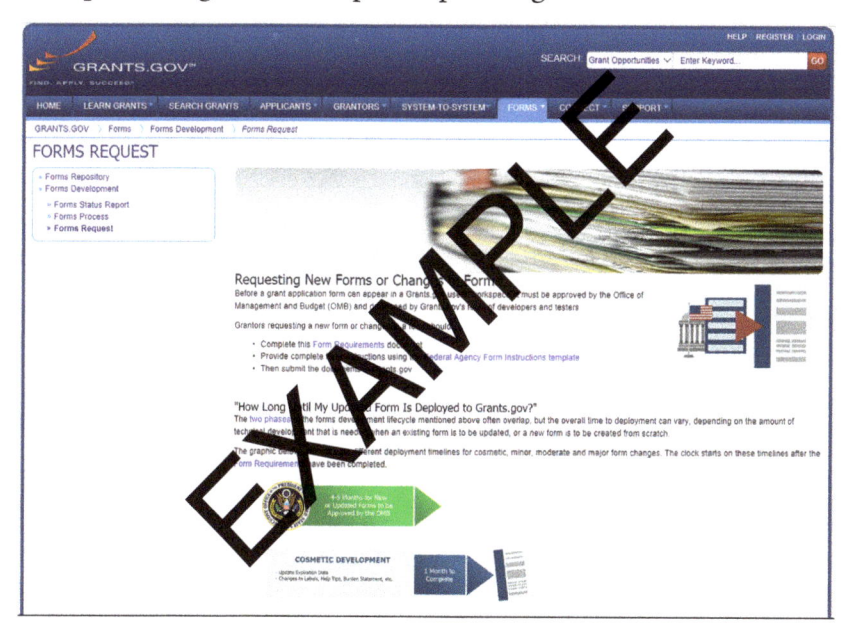

85

Ministry structure

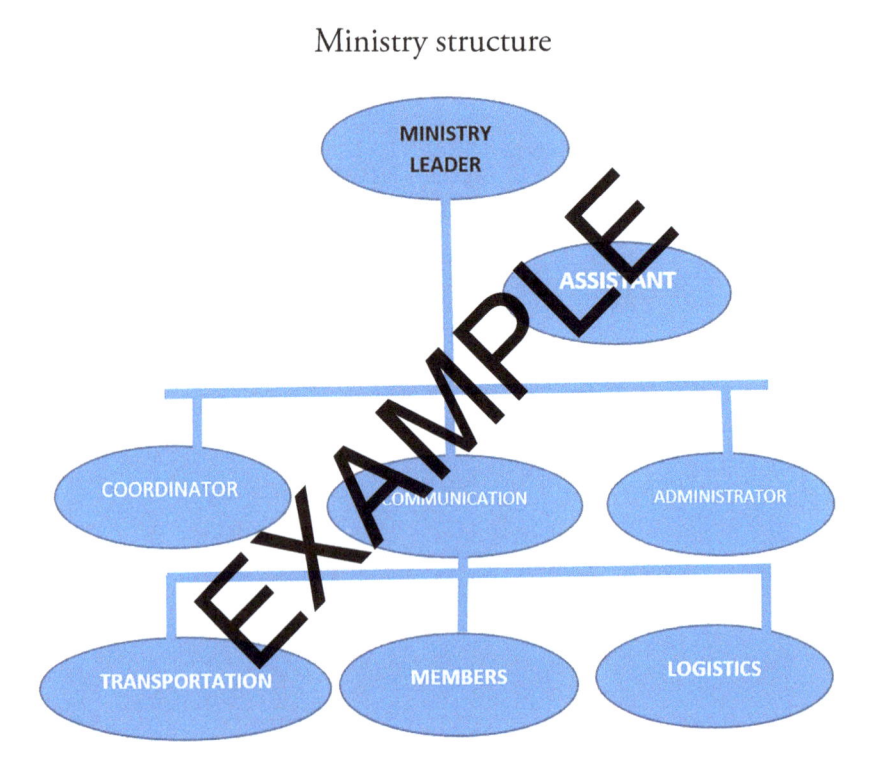

MY GRANDPARENTS

JONATHAN ARTHUR
07/27/1899 - 11/20/1972

MARTHA ARTHUR
10/10/1904 - 10/23/1989

Martha and Jonathan Arthur paved the way in making a part of my mission work easier than expected; they were missionaries in their way. They were considered monarchs in the family, and among them, they produced twelve children.

They owned a lot of lands and planted every inch of it with fruits, rice, and ground provision, and this food was their foundation, not only for their and their family's survival but for all those around them. There were also animals to take care of, and these are cows, chickens, and ducks.

My grandparents give most of their produce away, and they always had a helping hand for anyone who visited them and not forgetting that their home seemed to be a haven for anyone who wanted to stay overnight, which sometimes turn into weeks or longer.

My grandfather was a very tall man. He walked with ease and always looked as if he had a purpose every time he walked past me while I am sitting down, and to me, he looked like a tall king, especially when he was standing with his hands in his pocket looking up to the sky.

He spent most of his time on the farm, and he always had the time to help other farmers to plow or harvest their crops, for he seemed to have the only working machinery and equipment among the villagers. In addition to that, he was always helping someone who needed his assistance. I also remember him as a giver at heart and a man of little words.

I can say that he also gave his best, and it was shown especially during the harvest time. Every fruit and item that he gives to the church was the best out of his yielding in the field. They were without blemish, and he himself made sure they were delivered to *his* church.

He loved God and was diligent in his walk with Him, and he was also loved by many, especially his oldest daughter, Ermine. I am sure that all his children loved him because whenever I am among them, they never seem to stop talking about "Mother and Daddy."

They never spoke about one without the other, and after having a few conversations with a few of my aunts, I have a feeling that he was the person who came up with the idea of saying a Bible verse without looking at the Bible before going to bed!

However, through his hard work and devotion to his family, he kept everyone together, which includes his niece Vasil, and her brothers, Sherman, Sydney, Cedric, and Kelvin. This is due to the fact that my grandfather and his brother married my grandmother and her sister Kate.

In reference to my grandmother, she spent most of her time at home, taking care of the family; preparing the produce that had to be sold or given away; feeding the animals that were left behind, such as the cows that give milk and all the stray pets who show up in the yard.

I spent most of my time with my grandmother. During that period, my aunts, uncle, and cousins, and all the additional family and friends who were living at the house were gone, leaving a few of the grandchildren, including me, behind.

I remember my grandmother preparing to go to the market twice a week, and these days were Fridays and Saturdays, to sell fruits and produce. She would wake up very early in the morning on both days and travel to the market to sell the provision that she had taken and would return home late in the evening after a long day of shouting on the top of her voice. She would be yelling out all the different types of things that were in her cart for sale.

Sometimes, she would make my older sister and me go with her. It was a little embarrassing, at first, to sit at the back of the cart while my grandmother sits in the front of the cart steering the donkey, which was named Jobranner, away from the oncoming traffic.

Many children would run alongside and behind the cart, begging for pieces of fruit, and my grandmother would stop and share the fruits with them. She would look at their subtle faces and give those additional fruits and provision for them to take home to their families.

On rare occasions, I see my grandmother receive payments for the things she give away, and I am sure, with all her hard work, she gave away more fruits than she sold. For me, it was the satisfaction of making sure that the many fruits that grew on our land did not spoil or go to waste, and for her, judging from the amount of fruits she gave away, it was to make sure that the families were satisfied.

Despite her tiredness when she returned home, there was always a satisfaction on her face, and before going to bed, my grandmother would begin preparing for the next day. She would call my brother, Alston, to take care of the donkey, Jobranner, and funny enough, when someone calls the donkey by that name, he would respond by flexing his ears.

About the donkey, it appears that he was very stubborn and knew when it was time to leave for the market. The donkey would be grazing around the yard all week, and immediately, when it was time to go to the market, he would disappear, and he had many hiding places. My brother would sometimes spend half the night looking for the donkey, and he would find him and take him to the house and tie him up for the market, and the next week, everything begins all over again. One interesting factor it that this donkey knew where his home was. My grandmother will, sometimes, be asleep in the cart, and the donkey would take her directly home and stop in front of the house.

However, despite it all, my grandmother was a true missionary who did not know that she had touched many lives, especially those who ate either the fruits from the donkey cart or the food from her table, not forgetting her monthly activities of feeding the poor in the city, patronizing other business, and patronizing people like herself who were selling different goods to earn money, such as straw hats and straw handbags.

Now that all the children, including myself, are adults, I get the opportunity to listen to some of the people talk about how helpful the fruits and provisions were during their hungry times, and because of these forms of talks while on our mission trips, our missionary crew were welcomed in the home of some of the villagers to talk about Jesus Christ.

She had many names, but to me, she is Mothda, a true missionary at heart who did not know that because of her actions, many doors were opened to me and my mission counterparts for the word of God to spread.

As I looked at what she had done, I know that she was blessing to all those people while she was selling half and giving away half of her produce in her donkey cart. If she was preaching the gospel at the same time, one can imagine how many souls she would have saved and how many lives souls she would have drawn to Christ. Now here we are years later. Here I am, her granddaughter, spreading the gospel to the same people, their children, and grandchildren.

I can now say that this lasting legacy that my grandmother left behind paved a special way for me to continuously spread the Gospel to draw as many souls as possible to Christ and allowing me to becoming a true missionary for Christ, and with this I say, "Thank you, Mothda, the mother to everyone in the village who constantly sang and hum the song 'Blessed Assurance' as she worked!"

ERMINE EVELYN OLIVE

RUBY STEVEN STELLA

VIOLET PEARLEY FRANK

ELLEN PERCY EDNA

BECOMING A MISSIONARY

Nowhere in my life had I had plans to become a Christian missionary, and nowhere in my life had I had plans to serve GOD, even though I have lived among pastors, ministers, deacons, and many church members all my life.

To be frank, I felt that Christianity seemed to be too strict of a lifestyle, and this type of life would have cramped my so-called lifestyle. One of the reasons was because, in addition to learning my school works, there was one more daunting task before going to bed, and that was to remember and recite a memory verse from the bible, other than "Jesus wept" or "God is love" because those Bible verse were always taken by the older siblings.

My Bible during that time was the Harlequin romance books, not the Holy Bible. After reading a few of those books, I was hooked, and as immature as I was, I based my future life on what was written in the books, and my plans were to be, as one would say, "Be somebody," and God was nowhere in the midst of it. I was going to fall in love, get married to my prince charming who would sweep me off my feet, give birth to about two to three children, live in a very large white picket-fence home, have a generous career, retired before the age of fifty-five, and enjoyed life with my perfect little family. All in all, I forgot that fairy tales start with "Once upon a time" and ends with "Happily ever after," while man's life is full of twists and turns.

I am sure that I am not the only person who had that dream for themselves.

As I looked at myself in the mirror one day, in my hallway at home, I could see my hair balding from the top, and with gray hair on my head and eyebrows. I was surprised of what I became and soon began to remember all the dreams I had for myself. Not that I am unhappy, but reality hit home when I looked at my physical appearance, and suddenly, I realized that I have aged quite a bit.

I thank God that I was remembering the things that I could smile and laugh about because it was not a very good idea to allow oneself to think about the difficult times or the time that one was hurt, for that path would have taken me to a place of depression and pain, for that is a place God had brought me from.

I remember surrendering my life to Christ for a while when living in the country where I was born. I was attending church regularly, participating in all that the church was doing for the youth, becoming a youth minister, assisting in teaching Sunday school, and assisting in all the church programs. They were wonderful things to do, and I was enjoying myself, and also I was avoiding the tasks that my grandmother would give to me at home which needed to be done.

Years later, I migrated to the United States, where I joined the United States Armed Forces and, as one would say, "Took a break from God." Not that I was doing a lot of bad things that were not pleasing to God, just a little disobedience, and yes, I know that a sin is a sin regardless of how big or small, and during this period of time, I thought I was enjoying myself, however, nothing I planned for myself came to pass.

Falling in love was a failure from the beginning. Every man that spoke to me or show some form of attention to me, I absolutely knew they were the one I was going to be married to, and because of this, I ended up with two failed marriages. One would have thought that I would have learned not to do things myself without God, and many times after that, I did not learn. Through desperation, I turned to an old boyfriend because an individual in my position should have someone on my arms wherever I go.

I was planning to marry for the third and final time, reassuring myself this was the right person and the right thing to do, bearing in mind that God was nowhere in the plan. However, this person that I thought would marry me called me on his wedding night to say he was married. So I decided not to have any type of relationship for over thirteen years, until God blessed me with a man of God as my husband and two adoptive sons whom I call "my brats," and a grandchild who has the sharpest teeth in her mouth, who felt that the only place they can be sunk into is my arm.

When it came to my home, I thank God it only has three bedrooms because house cleaning would have been a great factor if I had got the large mansion I wanted. And when it came to my career, I am still asking myself if it was the best thing to join to United States Armed Forces, however, it was my safe haven and a blessing.

I rose to the rank from private to staff sergeant within six years, which was rare during my time as a chief administrative specialist. It allowed me to educate myself, earning various degrees and achieving many other certificates, and the positions afforded me to meet many nice and not so nice people. I was also able to live and visit various countries such as Germany, Russia, Italy, Spain, England, Guyana, South Africa, Greece, Barbados, Niger and, of course, the United States.

It was during the military phase, while living in Italy, that I came to my senses, and God sent my now mentor to me because

He saw the destructive path I was leading. I met Baby Perry in a small beach store. I was living at the beach during that time, and while heading home, I stopped at the store for the first time out of curiosity.

As I parked my car and walked into the store, immediately, as I entered, this woman called my name, "Sharon." And I said, "Baby?" I automatically knew who she was because her spouse, who worked with me at the Northern Atlantic Treaty Organization (NATO), spoke about her at our job and mostly because we were the only two people who were not Italians in the area. We held each other, walked out of the shop without buying anything, and drove off without knowing where we were going and ended up at the military commissary.

Later that night, after visiting the military and shopping centers, we went to her home, and I was introduced to her three beautiful daughters, and immediately after that, Baby sat in a chair and began praying, with tears in her eyes, thanking God. (To date, I never asked her why she was thanking God.)

At that moment, a feeling of guilt and shame came over me, and all I did was watch her for a while as she prayed with the tears running down her cheeks, praising God. I opened my mouth to speak, and all I could say was "Jesus."

That evening, God showed me that one does not have to have material things or food in your home for us to give Him all the praise, for there is that woman who did not have a lot to eat, waiting at a corner store, hoping to meet someone who can help her, worshiping God and thanking Him. Then she began to pray for me, and the very next day, I visited her home, and we prayed together and has never stopped praying since then.

QUESTION: Have you ever thought of what you would have liked to become when you were young, and did you achieve the goals?
DISCUSSION: _____
_____
_____
_____

MY SO-CALLED BREAK FROM GOD

During my so-called break from God, I experienced many unnecessary things. I got married twice, and both were for all the wrong reasons. I quit the first marriage because of lack of communication, and the second marriage, I thought I knew what I was getting myself into. But immediately after I said "I do," there was a change of attitude in both my spouse and me.

Every time he said something I did not like, I was answering him back with the same flourishing words that he used, and during this time, he was a strong Masonic member. I decided to join the organization with him, with the feeling that if we have something in common, things would get better; however it did not, but I continued in the organization which was known as the Eastern Stars, where I became a Worthy Matron and, later a Loyal Lady ruler. In both cases, I was reading the Bible, but for all the wrong reasons. I learned a lot, especially when it came to leadership, and gained great friendship and taught a lot about things not to do. To date, I can proudly say more than 90 percent of these women are serving the Lord in the way God wants them to do and are involved in some form of counseling.

I soon came to terms that my then-husband and me, had absolutely nothing in common, and the relationship reached to a point where we were walking past each other without speaking, and this continued until, one day, he seemed to be in a mood to pick a fight with me, and he began to call out names, such as rice-eating foreigner, and I was nothing but a barren cow, and no other man is going to want me, only him, so I better start talking to him.

Absolutely, yes, I eat rice every day, and no, I did not give birth to any children because of his decision, and I am sure I was pretty enough for someone else to have me, but he was not going to be the person to tell me those words. And as one says, "He got on my last nerve," and I answered him, and this time, he was not having it.

We physically fought. Imagine two soldiers who knew about all sorts of weapons, who knew how easy it is to bring a man to their knees fighting, and that day, I ended up with my face being smashed into a fish tank, causing me to be blind for a few months, and he ended up with probation, anger management class, and other little infractions.

Yet because of not focusing on God, I lean on every individual who would listen to me for their advice and ended up in counseling, only to find out that the counselor was one of my ex-spouse's friends!

At that time, I felt that I was being punished. I felt sorry for myself, ashamed because of my plans for me, had feelings of abandonment, feelings of rejection, that I have reached a delicate place in my life, and yes, it was all about me, how I feel. And even then, I did not pray to God.

I was driven with anger, hate, the feeling of letdown, the feeling of embarrassment because, at that time, I was an ROTC instructor, and nowhere this should have happened to me. I began to wonder what other people would say because I was only looking at the outward appearance.

Now one may ask why I did not pray. My answer would be, I was not thinking about praying; I was fighting my own battle.

Why I did not seek help? I did not know I needed it. I was taking care of the situation myself, and the more I lost, I was looking forward to winning

Did I blame myself? No, I threw all the blame at his feet because I did not care anymore, and I would get back at him for all that he has done to me.

Someone asked me if I felt suicidal, my answer was, No, this individual did this to me, I and have to get back at him!

With all of this, during that time, God was watching over me, and I was not paying Him any attention.

Now I can say, "God, I am a regenerated self," and I was touched by God and is just the vessel that He is using (Ephesian 3:7).

SPIRITUAL BIOGRAPHY, SHARON FORDE-ATIKOSSIE, DMIN

Missionary at heart, continuous learner, preacher, counselor, mentor, leader, administrator, organizer executive, community worker, and concerned for the needs of others are some of the things that I can sincerely describe myself as. My passion for learning and studying promotes a scholarly approach to both biblical and secular studies. I also have a passion for outreach ministries which allows me to preach the gospel on salvation regularly in the nursing homes, senior homes, charter schools, and orphanages, both in the Philadelphia community and internationally. I participate in Project Give at my secular job by volunteering at the low-income schools in the Philadelphia area, assisting young adults to achieve the highest goals in learning, teaches courses on ministry leadership, teaches church and secular etiquette, and assists in establishing foreign mission projects for other churches internationally.

I was born in Guyana, South America, and surrendered my life to Christ at the age of seventeen in Guyana, South America, and performed the duties as a Sunday school teacher, church board member, youth ministry leader, and also served on the choir ministry.

I migrated to the United States where I joined the United States Armed Forces and continue to serve the Lord through ministering, mentoring, and counseling to my peers and subordinates, not only in the secular world but also spiritually. I began participating in mission works in various countries such as England, Turkey, Italy, Greece, Czechoslovakia, Germany, Spain, Barbados, Guyana, South Africa, and West Africa, and is still doing so in Guyana, and Barbados.

In 2005, I retired from the military, returned to the United States, and resigned from my childhood church (AGAPE) in South America and joined Faith and Love Center Pentecostal Church, where myself and my family became members. I am currently serving as a Sunday school teacher, a ministry leader for both hospitality and outreach, Kingdom Kids assistant, Vacation Bible School director, UCF outreach mission, and in any other capacity when needed. I am blessed with my spouse Robert, his three children—Karen, Fabrice, Ako Paolo (Kevin)—and their grandbaby, London (Tele Fabriena).

In 2012, my family and me founded an organization, the Sharing of Bread Outreach Ministry, for the purpose of drawing souls to Christ and for reaching out to those in need through spiritual counseling, preaching, teaching, serving hot meals, giving rations to the homeless military veterans and to those in need within the city of Philadelphia and also serves raw rations and donates monies monthly to international countries.

I am currently a member of the America Counsel Association. I attended Columbia College, Ohio Christian University, Trident University, Grand Canyon University, United States Diplomat School of Etiquette, United States Armed Forces school for large- and small-room instructor certification, Mel Floyd School of Evangelism, and has completed various biblical courses from Faith and Love Center Pentecostal Church which included the 10 Steps to Christian Maturity. I achieved degrees and received numerous certificates in various topics about Christianity to do the works of the Lord.

MISSIONARY ONBOARD!

QUESTION: What are your achievements?
DISCUSSION: _____
_____
_____
_____

MY JOURNEY

Generally, there should be a foundation for missionaries. It should be mandatory that they go through some form of extensive studies about missions of the Word of God, thereby, understanding the concepts of God, understanding religious ideas and their nature, understanding the obedience of God, including getting the understanding of various types of cultures.

During my first short-term mission trip, I learned very quickly to adapt and learned the true meaning of the word COMPLEMENT. If a Christian missionary remembers this, in addition to the Word of the Lord, they would be able to accomplish the task, which is to draw souls to Christ.

It would be advisable to use the five Cs which I have learned to write on the front of my note pads, and these are:

- *Complement.* If this is done in the right manner, the responses that one would receive would be very receptive.
- *Complain.* Do not complain about unnecessary things, especially when you first arrive at the place of your mission.
- *Compare.* Do not compare your lifestyle to the host mission; be receptive, and it would be best to remind oneself of the mission at hand.

- *Condemn.* This type of action would send one home earlier than expected; a missionary is on a mission trip to do God's work.
- *Criticize.* Who are we to judge others?

When we look in the Bible, we see that it's stated in Luke 9:3. "And he said unto them, 'Take nothing for your journey, neither staves, nor scrip, neither bread, neither money; neither have two coats apiece'" (Luke 9:3).

To be honest, this Bible verse should be used depending on where one is going, such as traveling without a purse, for in today's society, in many places where missionaries go, there is a great physical and spiritual need.

No mission trip is the same. They are all different in many ways except for the reason for going, and it is to draw God's children closer to Him and to see how God is working through His children, and as I continue to be obedient to God, He guided me through the difficult times and the best of times.

I learned that keeping an open mind is good for a missionary because there is always the unexpected situation that will occur, and when standing firm on the Word of God and obeying the character that God wants us to have so that we can deal with many situation.

MY MISSION TRIP EXPERIENCES

During my twenty years in the United States Armed Forces, I had completed a total of twenty-five mission trips with various churches, ranging from weekend trips to one week yearly trips, and on every trip, different items were taken to assist the people in need, and it was interesting to observe how compassionate and thankful most of the people were.

I felt that those missionaries who went before me had prepared a groundwork so that our operations would go smoothly. This is because we were always welcome, and preparations were already there. Also, everything seemed to be in order upon arrival, and because of this, I looked forward to returning or looked forward to going on another mission. There was also that feeling of wanting to help and preaching the gospel.

After retiring from the United States Armed Forces, I continued to do God's work within my neighborhood and was given the opportunity to focus on longer mission trips, focusing on one or two places.

During my first mission trip, a total of five long cold days, I listened to the direction and instructions of the mission leader, however, because of my ignorance, I suffered a bit. We were heading to Czechoslovakia, and on this journey, I found myself in the coldest place on earth where there was no heat. Upon observation, everyone was wearing animal skins which had a very high odor. The people did not want to hear about God; all they wanted was the food that the director had for them.

The church we visited had only one bench, and there was no electricity. There was a heap of coals with lukewarm heat, with open windows all around. The pastor had a candle which quickly blew out, and he was continually scratching matches to keep lighting it, and during all this time, I was cold from head to toe. My feet were burning, and my body was shivering, and during this time, the people were lining up outside the church for something to eat.

As they drifted through the line to get their small bag of peas, rice, and other small items, I can see the pain in some of their eye and the great fullness in some. Some of the women had their babies under their clothes to keep them warm, and for me, I did not realize that the additional cold I was feeling on my face was from the uncontrollable tears that were constantly flowing down my cheeks.

After sharing the food, I thought they all would have left to go where they came from, but most of them stuck around to hear the word of God spoken in their languages, and I was astonished to see them praising God, despite not having anything, and in the midst of this, I was jumping up and down worshiping Him and did not feel the cold until the service was over, and we began to pack to return to Germany. And during my traveling, I prayed to God to give me the strength and courage to continue to serve Him in whatever way He wants me to because I see His wonders despite the physical struggle. I saw the calmness the people had in their faces despite their hunger and needs, and I wanted some of that feeling of calmness, and this was when my missionary trips began while in the military to present.

Returning to Guyana

At one point, I felt that I was being punished because I was led to the country where I was born (Guyana, South America).

The family and friends had already heard that I had "backslid," and one can imagine some of the insulting letters and notes I had received, and not forgetting, when I would make a call to say hello, it included comments such as, "I knew you would not turn out to be anything," and because of this and other situations, I stayed away from everyone for about thirteen years except for my immediate family which included my mother, sisters, and brothers.

Returning home to spread the Gospel the first time was not easy. The feeling of nervousness allowed me to feel sick all over my body, and because of my nervousness, I asked the leader to send me to another church where no one knows me for I was not prepared to face the "firing squad,' so I thought.

Unfortunately for me, I was tasked to go and minister to my home church for one night, and the sermon I had prepared the night before for a youth service would not have worked. I was picked up by my former pastor and his spouse, and the only conversation that was said was greeting each other. And as we approached the church, I got a feeling of sickness in my stomach and another feeling that the pastor did not need me there. He suspected how I felt, and his comment to me was, "This is what you get when you do not communicate, and the last time I heard, you were not living a godly life." I wanted to jump out of the car, but luck would have it we reached the church.

As I walked in on trembling feet, there was a quietness in the place, and that was for two reasons, for I had gained an extra 170, and the other was I was a backslider. This was a time I wished my husband was with me. However, as I sat in front of the church, I heard a clap, and then everyone began clapping. I folded my fingers in the palm of my hand and squeezed as hard possible so as not to cry. It was one of my cousins who began to clap, and when I turned around, I was very much relieved to see the surprise and smiles on the people's faces.

The pastor took the pulpit, and instead of introducing me, he took the opportunity to call out everyone's name whom he had not seen in church for a long time, and of course, the majority of them were my friends and a few cousins.

My preaching became a forum of discussion, question, and answers, and after a while, I did not realize that I was not nervous anymore, and the pastor, the seriousness on his face changed to a smile. I think he was happier than he saw a crowded church on a Wednesday night, however, I was welcome to return anytime to preach at his church.

Another visit to Guyana allowed me to visit the village where I was born, and while standing at the pulpit, the first person my eyes came into contact with was one of the mothers of the church, whose fruits trees my friends and I used to climb and steal her fruits from when we were children, and during the discomfort, the topic of my sermon became "Thou shall not steal," rather than "How wonderful it is to surrender to Christ."

DOING TOO MUCH

As we surrender our lives to Jesus Christ, even though our primary responsibility is to always be in an evangelism mode, we are also blessed with various gifts that were given to us through the Holy Spirit, and sometimes, we forget that they are not gifts for ourselves to selfishly hold on to but to use it for the kingdom of God in order for us to reach lost souls and draw them to Christ.

I am often told that I am working too hard or doing too much, and I always ask myself what is too much for the Lord, or how much is too much, when I know, without Him, I would not have a breath in my body. And one day, I challenged myself to honestly give an account of how many newborn souls I am responsible to bring to Christ, either in the church or during mission trips, and to examine my behavior and character.

When it comes to honestly giving an account of how many newborn souls we were responsible to bring to Christ, either in the church or during mission trips, my answer is three to four individuals within the last two years, and if doing so on my own, I can sincerely say only one individual. This answer may astonish many and may even draw criticism, for how can I be a leader and a child of God and not do the main things that God wants from me, and that is to reach out to His children and tell them about Him in a manner in which they would be interested to want to know more about who Jesus is.

I not only realized but acknowledge that there is a lot of room for correction and improvement on my part, especially when looking at the below information which show that within 365 days, I am spending about 178 days either interacting, having or attending meetings, preaching to, speaking to, solving situations, and socializing with individuals who have already surrendered their lives to Christ, or as an old soldier would say, "is already in the system."

Yes, I do attend a church that has an evangelism ministry, however, it is my responsibility to reach lost souls, and not forgetting that the ministry will not meet the people where I attend work, go shopping, or even in my travels.

AM I REACHING LOST SOULS

After looking at the chart, there seems to be no room to evangelize or to reach anyone. This is not because I forgot, it is because of the excuses that I can make, such as the fact that I drive to work each day and do not meet any new people, when I return home I am too tired, or by the time I finished my house chores and schoolwork, it is late to reach out to people. Or I can justify my behavior and say that when I wake up in the morning, I pray for myself, giving thanks to God, and pray that all those around me for them to have the heart to seek God.

ACTIVITIES	AVERAGE DAYS PER YEAR
Actual evangelism without going with the ministry	5
Organization feeding	12
Organization interaction	24
Attending church Sundays	35
UCF meetings	3
Serving meals	12
Hospitality ministry meetings	9
Outreach ministry meeting	12
Outreach preaching	15
Vacation Bible School	5
Kingdom Kids	5
Pastor retreat	1

Women retreat	1
Conferences/second services/ other meetings; guest chef	20
International travels	14

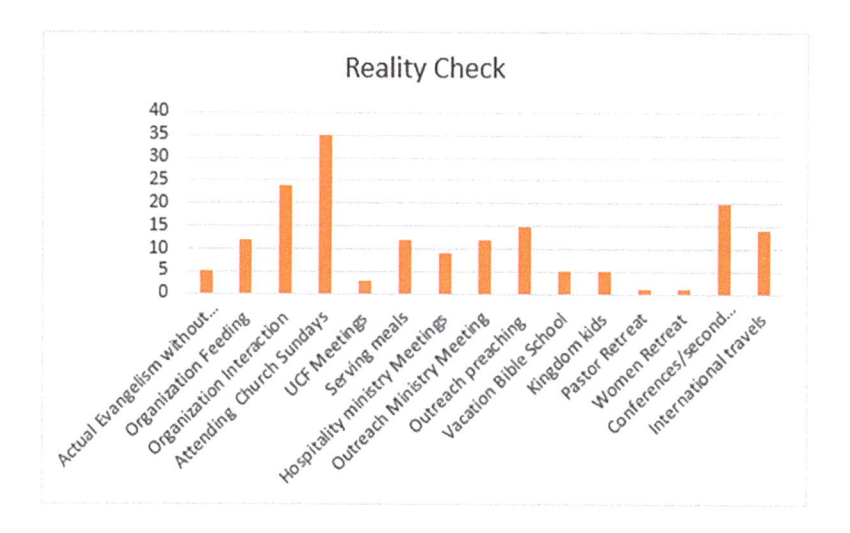

Reality Check

(Bar chart showing values for: Actual Evangelism without..., Organization Feeding, Organization Interaction, Attending Church Sundays, UCF Meetings, Serving meals, Hospitality ministry Meetings, Outreach Ministry Meeting, Outreach preaching, Vacation Bible School, Kingdom kids, Pastor Retreat, Women Retreat, Conferences/second..., International travels)

My conclusion is not to stop my activities but to fix that which is broken, which is to find a way to reach lost souls, and this can be done by simply taking the bus to work at least once a week and not forgetting to seek God for the boldness to hand out cards with information about Jesus Christ, which includes information about a church that they can attend.

Another way would be, when shopping, to stop and tell people about the Lord, just as other religions are doing, and when on international travels, continue to spread the Gospel of Jesus Christ and, in some cases, depending on where I am, attract the audience to come to me by giving out water, snacks, or even hot meals or sandwiches.

When looking at my behavior and character, they both are tied in with my secular life and spiritual life, and considering the fact that due to my secular job, I have to take spontaneous and yearly polygraph test. I have no choice in this matter; however, that does not exclude me from inappropriate behavior from time to time, not deliberately. I learned that when I thought my behavior was right, I found out that it was wrong and, of course, offended many, and soon realized that my behavior can be defined as the way I act and react to various situation.

In the case of my character, I see it as my qualities that are inside of me. It is my values, my ethics, and my morale and my actions, all of which, God created in me.

QUESTION: Have you ever experienced this or something similar?
DISCUSSION:_____
_____
_____
_____

MY EXPERIENCE RETURNING HOME AS A MISSIONARY

After returning to my childhood home after many years, everything seemed different. I began searching for my childhood friends and only found one them, and her name is Rita Headley. We chatted for a while and promised to keep in contact, and we did. I began sending her little videos of preaching, and to God be the glory, she surrendered her life to Jesus Christ, and became a member of one of the churches in one of the villages.

When I looked at the neighbor's fruit trees, I was shocked to see them still bearing fruits, and the trees looked the same way when I left them in 1984 as I migrated to the United States. You see, these trees were my toys to play with. As a child, I would climb them, swing from branch to branch, and pick the fruits off of them without permission.

I came to realize that the trees have their life cycle, and they do not die easily. Their leaves fall and drop to the ground and wither, then more leaves would spring up. Sometimes, before the leaves fall, small leaves would begin to sprout, and this is the cycle of the trees, and so it is for mankind.

When it comes to climbing the trees, one cannot reach the top that easily. They cannot climb straight to the top. There is always the matter of choosing the right branches to hold on to, and even when one reaches the top, they have to hold on to many branches in order not to fall.

When I looked at my life that has so many twists and turns, I realized that man will always need help from others, regardless of what they are doing, just as how I needed stronger branches or a collection of not so strong branches to get to the top of the trees.

The top of the tree can be represented as a form of leadership role. The leader, as everyone knows, is located at the top, and when we think about a pyramid, we can see where the leader should be. In the secular environment, the leader has the authority to direct and give orders, without getting support from their subordinate or those below them, because there is this sense of production-driven environment.

In the case of the spiritual environment, we will find that at the bottom or below the leaders is the congregation who are the supporters for the pastors, for without the congregation, there is no one for the pastor to preach to, and church is not a one-man gig. The congregation plays a very important role, and without them, there are no missions. So the pastors and the congregation has important parts to make us a body of Christ.

QUESTION: Have you ever compared anything to man's life achievement?

DISCUSSION: _____
_____
_____
_____

THE WORD FAITH

Fully Aligning In True Holiness

I participated at a leadership luncheon among some Christian leaders, and during the luncheon, everyone was asked to write down a word that fits them. I paused for a while, and I found myself writing down the word *faith*.

I pondered over the word that I wrote down and immediately wondered why I wrote it. I knew that I trust God, I knew that I believe in Him, and also knew that, from experience, it is because of faith that I succeeded in many of my missions, and it is also the results of my request of the things I prayed and asked Him for. I also knew that I must wait on Him to answer and, regardless of what it may be, still get satisfaction of loving Him and believing in Him even if the answer is no.

I also know that I have been releasing the steering wheel of my life and letting Him do the driving for me. (To be honest, sometimes, I wanted to do the driving myself and is still in the process of not wanting to release totally.)

I went to my room, and as I sat quietly, my husband asked the question, "What is it this time?" I said the word faith is on my mind, and we began to write down all the meanings of faith.

Faith is: believing, trusting, belief and confidence, surrendering.

Am I doing all of these things all the time? And the answer is no, and since I have been honest with myself, I am recognizing the areas of my character that needs to be improved, especially if I am doing the work of the Lord.

My faith is knowing that I was touched by God and that I am just the vessel of God and believe that He called me for an assignment that is bigger than what I thought it would be.

QUESTION: What do you suggest *faith* is?
DISCUSSION: _____
_____
_____
_____

MISSIONARY WALK WITH GOD

A missionary walk with God is not as straightforward as one may think; there are many twist and turns, especially for those missionaries who travel overseas.

One important aspect of a missionary is that they must be careful of their intention and remember that drawing lost souls to Christ is their priority, and the physical need of the people comes after.

As human beings, it is very easy for one to feel sorry for another who is in need or is in a difficult position, for the Bible tell us in Matthew 28:19, "Therefore go and make disciples of all nations, baptizing them in the name of the Father and of the Son and the Holy Spirit."

- The missionary meets different types of people with different personalities.
- The missionary will not be in agreement with everyone.
- Not everyone will appreciate what the missionary is doing.
- Some people will try to make the missionary works for the Lord difficult by saying untruthful things about it.
- There are individuals who would continuously condemn the missionary.
- Some people will assume the worst of the missionary and act on it.
- Some people would not trust the missionary.

- There are those who would criticize what the missionaries are doing.
- Some will invoke mistrust about the missionary to others.
- Some will provide false information to others about the missionary so that they are unable to succeed in their works of the Lord.
- There are those who would express to others that the missionary is not of God.
- There are those who would question the missionary's motive.

I am sure that many leaders have experienced these types of treatments, but when we look at Jesus Christ, all of these things occurred to him, and yet He pressed on. When it comes to pressing on, sometimes a missionary can get discouraged and hurt; however, they must remember that when it comes to serving the Lord, there will always be a distraction.

A prime example is Jesus. He was a missionary at heart, and we see this in His life on earth. He traveled all over and spread the Gospel. Not only that, He preached the gospel, he did many miracles, teaching, healing, feeding, and He ended up dying on the cross for mankind.

When looking at the New Testament, one will see the validation of how Jesus was treated, especially those who were close to him. Some respected him, some trusted him, some love him, some believe in Him, yet with all that He did, there were those who showed anger, showed distrust, showed hatred, encouraged others to not love him, and what's most hurtful is that there were those whom He fed and healed but did not continue to live for Him.

THE DEVIL MADE ME DO IT!

Every Christian knows that there is an adversary who would try to devour them, and they must always stay close to God and not give that adversary the opportunity for them to use the following statements, especially missionaries: "The devil made me do it," "The devil used me," "They allowed the devil to use them."

These are statements that many leaders hear within the body of Christ, and as a missionary, I overhear this statement at least twice a week, either at church or in the secular environment.

I have used this phrase many times in the past; however, after learning that it was not a good idea to give the devil any credit for my actions when I knowingly did wrong, I decided to take the responsibility for my action and try to think before I say or do anything.

These statements are excuses for an individual to behave nastily and wickedly. There are some who use these comments so that they can have that feeling of satisfaction and power in order to be insulting, to be very manipulative, to be cunning, and to be selfish toward others. All of these are examples of being a snake, and when those around them behave in this manner, one would find themselves not knowing who to trust. But we must rely on God's guidance only and for the adversary not to play a part in our lives.

I am not a pastor as yet, but I learned not to say what I would not do; however, from a leadership standpoint, when dealing with a snake, one has to be prayerful, especially the pastors, who have the responsibility of an entire congregation. This is a topic which pastors and leaders do not want to address for there is a fear of losing their members, especially since they will have to operate as a doctor in a hospital, which means, when cutting out cancer from your body, the doctor cannot take all the cancer out without touching and cutting the flesh that are not infected., and this is a form of sacrifice some pastors do not want to make.

These statements affect the missionaries in a different way. They must remember that evil company will corrupt good men. In saying this, missionaries do not only deal with those that are saved; they deal with the unsaved and can easily get distracted, especially when dealing with other cultures.

DIFFERENCE IN CULTURE

As stated before, when dealing with various cultures, it is not as easy as one would expect. It is always a work in progress to try to understand another language and another way of doing things.

For example, my spouse is from Togo, West Africa, my sons were born in Niger, West Africa, and I was born in Guyana, South America. We all migrated to the United States, where none of us understood the culture. It was difficult to speak English at home; my husband spoke French. He knew some English, I spoke broken British English, and my sons spoke no English.

We visited a few churches, and we were welcomed in a lukewarm manner on some occasions. We were faced with many questions, such as, "What do you want from the church?" "When can we take you out for a good meal?, "If you are coming for money, we do not have."

Another comment received is, "How many more of you all are coming because you people always come in droves," not forgetting another statement, "What qualifies you to be a pastor or a teacher?"

In most cases, my husband and I would smile, and if he is holding my hands, he would be squeezing it tightly in order for me to shut up, not forgetting the anger in both my sons. Even up to the present, my older son uses these comments as an excuse for not attending church.

As a pastor and a minister, and also missionaries, after traveling to so many places as missionaries, we were used to this type of statements and more; however, to God be the glory, we never allowed these forms of behavior stop us from serving God and spreading the Gospel.

We continue to attend classes and visited with many associate churches to get a better understanding of what to do and what not to do in order to be at peace with ourselves in the Lord.

I did not realize that I needed a degree to be qualified to attend certain churches other than being a saved and sanctified as a child of God; however, it does not hurt to have a degree or other form of documentation for validation, especially when travelling.

It is still a work in progress, and by placing God in the driving seat, He allows me to overcome any form of rejection, while our faith continues to become stronger in Him.

INEQUALITY TREATMENT OF THE MISSIONARY

Let us not be fooled that all missionaries are treated the same. I can only speak upon my observation and experience. I will advise any missionary that prior to travelling, they must make sure that the receiving country becomes aware of who they are, especially when it comes to their gender and their race. This action will eliminate all surprises and embarrassment.

During my travels, not all my experience was pleasurable, especially when meeting some people of my own skin color. As a black foreign missionary, in many cases, I was treated, as one would say, as politically correct. In some cases, my skin color was a factor, or the way I spoke was another factor. Sometimes, it did not matter, and in some cases, it did.

In the West African region, where the population was predominantly dark skinned, they are not accustomed to seeing someone like me as a missionary. There is the perception that only the light-skinned people are missionaries. When looking back at history, one would see the reason why. As stated before, in some countries, there are not a lot of missionaries with dark skin, and because of this, there is the misconception that they may be the maid for the lighter-skinned counterparts and will be treated as such.

For me, during my travels, as the leader of a certain group where I was the only dark-skinned person, I was treated with respect, not because I demanded it but because of the respect of my qualification and knowledge and the fact that I lived before in the area where we were going as a soldier. At the airport, I was welcomed with a smile and assistance with my luggage, was escorted to my sleeping quarters, and was given a welcoming walk through.

On another mission, despite the fact that the official knew who I was, they demanded that I present additional credentials other than my passport and medical card, to prove that I am a missionary. On another occasion, the host country helpers refused to take my bags because they thought I was a maid.

The most difficult event was returning home, especially to the people who knew me as a child and growing up. I was recognized at the airport, and before long, everyone was visiting the hotel just to take a look at what I have become. Then there was the shock and disbelief that I was no longer the brat who climbed trees and stole fruits from the neighbors, and this is the time where great appreciation for my grandmother came to mind because there was the constant talks of missing her and the cart with mangoes. My grandmother, Martha Arthur, I can sincerely say, had paved a way for me to be accepted in the village where I was born.

However, to avoid these experiences and a lot more, it would be advisable to avoid ignorance. It would be a very good ideas to do the following:

* I made sure I have on hand the small wallet-size degrees, license, and certificate cards that were given to me by my university and other schools, my minister license, my mission license, the largest Bible in my hand.
* If I am the ministry leader, I have everyone's passport and place mine on top, along with a key ring full of different degrees and certifications, making sure that

we is meeting us knows who is the coordinator for the mission.

There is the issue of being a woman in position when dealing with various cultures, and to avoid any embarrassment, it is wise that the host country knows who they will be meeting and dealing with.

We must remember that not everyone we meet and have to work with are spiritually filled, and this is the reason a missionary should always be on alert and able to deal with various situations.

PREPARING FOR MY MISSION TRIP

Thank God for the training at Mel Floyd School of Evangelism and being allowed to volunteer at Chosen 300 Ministry, listening to the first lady of Antioch Community Church about her experiences, observing the pastors and their congregation perform their outreach missions at Grace Tabernacle, and thanks to an understanding bishop from the church where I attend who does not mind when I visit other churches and ministries as long as I notify him, and not forgetting all the conversation I have had with the saints of our church who experienced some form of ministering to or evangelizing to people.

These are the people and places where I visited prior to going on my mission trips in order to get a refresher course on how to deal with different cultures of people and to continue to learn additional approaches to evangelizing.

Best of all, I learned an easier way to evangelize while attending a class called "I Believe."

QUESTION: What other rules do you think you can use?
DISCUSSION: _____
_____
_____
_____

Knowing your lane as a missionary

Prior to going on any type of missionary trips, it is imperative that the missionary research everything about their destination. They should not depend on the mission leader. Again, the missionary needs to find out everything about the trip such as the geography, requirements, language, type of culture, whether they are going to the city or in the rural areas, find out if there are tribes to visit, what types of clothing the people wear.

For example, if a missionary knows that they cannot control their body if they see men, women, and children without clothing, then they should not go to mission trips where there are tribes who wear little or no clothing.

CONCLUSION

I love being a missionary and a child of God. It gives me the opportunity to see the works of the Lord firsthand not only in my life but to those around me. I learned that missionaries must always keep praying, they must always stay focused, and place God first in everything that they are doing. They must be able to listen when the Holy spirit is talking to them, always remain Christlike at all times, regardless of where they are and what they are doing. They should be resourceful by learning various forms of activities so that they can assist the locals. They should know when to speak up and when to shut up and should seek God's guidance ALWAYS and, best of all, draw souls to Jesus Christ!

REFERENCES

Ferris, Robert W. ed. May 6, 2018. *Establishing Ministry Training*.
Green, Keith. 1999, *The Ministry Years*.
Harley, David. June 27, 2012. *Preparing to Serve. Holy Bible*.
Lum, Ada. June 2, 1984. *A Hitchhiker's Guide to Missions*.
Wagner, C. Peter. Jan 1, 1972. *Frontiers in Missionary Strategy*.

ABOUT THE AUTHOR

Dr. Sharon Forde-Atikossie is a missionary, an instructor, and a retiree of the Unites States Armed Forces who has served, and is serving, the Christian church in many capacities since 1980s. She is a publisher and is the founder of The Sharing of Bread Outreach Mission and also the founder of Culture and Etiquette Office.

Printed in the USA
CPSIA information can be obtained
at www.ICGtesting.com
LVHW070007310723
753625LV00019B/541

9 781098 027032